LORD

IT'S ME AGAIN

JUDSON CORNWALL

LORD
IT'S ME AGAIN

BRIDGE PUBLISHING
South Plainfield, NJ

Lord, It's Me Again by Judson Cornwall
ISBN 0-88270-666-7
Library of Congress Catalog Card Pending
Copyright © 1994 by Judson Cornwall

Published by:
Bridge Publishing Inc.
2500 Hamilton Blvd.
South Plainfield, NJ 07080

To Mary Lou Flores,
my wife's sister, my Savior's daughter,
and my friend.

Other Bridge titles available by

Judson Cornwall

The Best of Judson Cornwall
Elements of Worship
Heaven
Let Us Abide
Let Us Be Holy
Let Us Draw Near
Let Us Enjoy Forgiveness
Let Us Praise
Let Us See Jesus
Let Us Worship
Profiles of a Leader

Available at Christian bookstores everywhere,
or write us:

Bridge Publishing, Inc.
P.O. Box 257
South Plainfield, NJ 07080

CONTENTS

Preface

Excitedly, my wife ripped open the large envelope from our granddaughter. It contained the latest picture of a great-grandson, and I was quickly sent to find a frame for it. While searching for just the right one, I saw a small poster with a photo of a little tiger peering over a tree limb with a wistful look in its eyes. Over the picture was the caption, *Lord, It's Me Again.* It so arrested my attention that I purchased it, framed it, and mounted it on the wall in my study along with the framed covers of the books I have written.

The poster has moved me to prayer more times than I can recount. Day after day, I have identified with that cry, for I desperately need to return to the Lord on a multiple daily basis. After several persons had mistaken this poster for a book cover, it occurred to me that the feelings and thoughts it had stirred in me might also inspire others to come again into God's presence.

I have experienced a very different set of emotions in writing this book. I don't know if I have identified with this truth more than some others I have written, or if I feel that I am sharing something that has been rather private for a year or more. All I know is that I have often had to pause in my writing to wipe away tears, and sometimes have powered-down my computer to have another season of prayer before continuing my writing.

I am still amazed at how easily I can be prevented from coming into God's presence with my whole being. I often compartmentalize myself — bringing portions of me into His presence while leaving other portions out. While my spirit revels in God's nearness, I find my mind wants to wander into the territory to be covered that day. I find secret compartments in my heart that tend to close the doors when I draw near to God, and yet these are the very areas of my life that need the energizing and, oftentimes, the cleansing that God's nearness brings.

Lord, It's Me Again is not a request to enter, but a polite statement informing the Lord that we have entered. It also speaks of repetition, for this entering is not new. It has been done many times, but it is being done again.

I urge the readers to not be dissuaded from reading the book because I have tied it to the Prodigal Son. This book is not an attempt to exegete that parable. I did that years ago in my book *Profiles of a Leader*. I have simply used this familiar story to form a structure for this book. Perhaps no one in the Bible is better known for returning home again than this son that Jesus told about. It is also likely that Jesus told no parable that we relate to more easily than the story of the Prodigal Son. It is a dramatic portrayal of God's words to Israel through the prophets:

> I will give them an heart to know me, that I am the LORD: and they shall be my people, and I will be their God: for they shall return unto me with their whole heart. . . . Return unto me, and I will return unto you, saith the LORD of hosts. (Jeremiah 24:7; Malachi 3:7)

Perhaps all of us need to stop playing ball [or feeding pigs] in the vacant lot next door and look over the fence into God's vast back yard. Is there anything in our surroundings that equals the beauty of His habitation? I urge you, the reader, to join me in looking over the fence with that wistful look and saying to Jesus, *Lord, It's Me Again.*

The Story of the Prodigal

Luke 15:11-32

And he said, A certain man had two sons:

And the younger of them said to his father, Father, give me the portion of goods that falleth to me. And he divided unto them his living.

And not many days after the younger son gathered all together, and took his journey into a far country, and there wasted his substance with riotous living.

And when he had spent all, there arose a mighty famine in that land; and he began to be in want.

And he went and joined himself to a citizen of that country; and he sent him into his fields to feed swine.

And he would fain have filled his belly with the husks that the swine did eat: and no man gave unto him.

And when he came to himself, he said, How many hired servants of my father's have bread enough and to spare, and I perish with hunger!

I will arise and go to my father, and will say unto him, Father, I have sinned against heaven, and before thee,

And am no more worthy to be called thy son: make me as one of thy hired servants.

And he arose, and came to his father. But when he was yet a great way off, his father saw him, and had compassion, and ran, and fell on his neck, and kissed him.

And the son said unto him, Father, I have sinned against heaven, and in thy sight, and am no more worthy to be called thy son.

But the father said to his servants, Bring forth the best robe, and put it on him; and put a ring on his hand, and shoes on his feet:

And bring hither the fatted calf, and kill it; and let us eat, and be merry:

For this my son was dead, and is alive again; he was lost, and is found. And they began to be merry.

Now his elder son was in the field: and as he came and drew nigh to the house, he heard musick and dancing.

And he called one of the servants, and asked what these things meant.

And he said unto him, Thy brother is come; and thy father hath killed the fatted calf, because he hath received him safe and sound.

And he was angry, and would not go in: therefore came his father out, and intreated him.

And he answering said to his father, Lo, these many years do I serve thee, neither transgressed I at any time thy commandment: and yet thou never gavest me a kid, that I might make merry with my friends:

But as soon as this thy son was come, which hath devoured thy living with harlots, thou hast killed for him the fatted calf.

And he said unto him, Son, thou art ever with me, and all that I have is thine.

It was meet that we should make merry, and be glad: for this thy brother was dead, and is alive again; and was lost, and is found.

1

Lord, It's Me, Hungering Again

A Change of Circumstances

You couldn't buy a job, homelessness was rampant, and the utility companies had cut off their services from many homes for non-payment of bills long past due. It was the winter of 1929, and America was in the tight grip of the Great Depression. With little else to turn to, many persons turned to God for solace and security.

The small and new congregation in Ukiah, California, could afford to rent an upstairs hall in the downtown district only on Sundays, so the mid-week prayer meeting was held in the home of the pastor — my father. Each person brought a piece of wood with him or her to contribute to heating the home for the evening. Those who attended either walked or came in carpools. Although gasoline was only ten cents a gallon, it was a dime more than they had available.

On this Wednesday night, I had been put to bed before the little flock of faithful believers arrived for prayer. The excitement of the gathering penetrated the walls between the front room and my bedroom, and I slipped out of bed and got on my knees to pray along with them. Although I was only five years old, I had already had a personal confrontation with Jesus and knew that I was saved.

While praying, the Lord Jesus gave me a vision of a suffering, dying world and then impressed me that He wanted me to go into this world and preach the Gospel. The experience was so real that I emptied a paper bag that stood in the corner of the room, and hastily put some of my clothes in it. I dressed myself in my Sunday best, picked up my packed bag and walked through the room of praying people while heading for the front door.

Stretching to reach the doorknob, I squeezed the bag. The crisp rustling noise the bag made aroused my mother's attention. As she looked up from her posture in prayer she said, rather sharply, "Judson, where do you think you are going?"

"Jesus just told me that I have to go into the world to preach the Gospel," I answered. "Good-bye, Mommy. Good-bye, Daddy. I have to obey Jesus."

With the wisdom that God gives to parents, mother said, "All right, Judson. If Jesus told you to go preach, we understand. But your father and I think that you should stay with us for a little longer and let us teach you more about Jesus and His love."

This made sense to me, and I stayed with my parents until time to leave for college. My vision and call were accurate. It was my timing that was off. I needed much more maturity before I was able to step into God's call. I needed to learn that between God's call and His commission is His college. I needed training.

Jesus told a story with a similar plot, but with a very different ending. It is a time-honored allegory that captures the attention of Christians and non-believers alike. The title of the story has made its way into our English vocabulary — the Prodigal Son. There are many Bible words that need to be clearly defined before their meanings are understood, but *prodigal* is not one of those words. The classic story Jesus told about the Prodigal Son is known in and out of religious circles, because everyone can relate to one or more of the four main characters. It is the story of a young man with a vision that reached far beyond his father's farm. He asked to receive his inheritance immediately so he could go out into the world and "do his thing." Jesus does not indicate that his motives were impure. Even the prodigal's father does not say that his son's actions were so wrong. The charge that he wasted all of his substance on riotous living was levied by his angry older brother. Whether this was true or not is not the point of the story.

The Prodigal Son simply wanted to be on his own before he was sufficiently mature to manage on his own. That he did mishandle his inheritance is evident when we see him, a Jew, employed in feeding pigs and so hungry that he shared their food with them. His self-will created a serious change of circumstances for him. He, like we, had received much from the father, but he had to return to the father for survival.

It's Me, Hungry Again

How often do we take what our heavenly Father shares with us and run out to do our own thing? In our spiritual immaturity, we waste all our spiritual substance and find it impossible to survive spiritually. We have to face the necessity of returning to Father and saying, "Lord, it's me again. I'm hungry."

No one likes to be hungry, but hunger is a very real problem in our world. Those of us who live in the affluence of America know little about hunger, though we have thousands of homeless, hungry people living in our cities. Unfortunately, our ignorance of the facts does not change the circumstances of the less fortunate. Extreme famine conditions have plagued the world of mankind from biblical times until now. Entire races of people have disappeared from the face of the earth as the result of famines.

What is true in the natural is also true in the spiritual. Church history shows that generations of people have lacked sufficient spiritual food. The prophet Amos wrote:

> Behold, the days come, saith the Lord GOD, that I will send a famine in the land, not a famine of bread, nor a thirst for water, but of hearing the words of the LORD: And they shall wander from sea to sea, and from the north even to the east, they shall run to and fro to seek the word of the LORD, and shall not find it. (Amos 8:11-12)

It is difficult to imagine a spiritual famine in America since we have an abundance of churches, Christian radio stations, and nationwide Christian telecasts. No country in the world has as many Christian bookstores as does America. Several hundred new Christian books come off the presses each year, and Gospel music is available in abundance. Still, a mere profusion of food does not prevent starvation. There must be a willingness to gather, prepare and eat that food before it is of any value. It is not what is in our cupboards that prevents hunger; it is what is in our stomachs.

When Israel first came out of Egypt, God deliberately let them experience natural hunger to teach them spiritual lessons. The sacred historian wrote:

> He humbled thee, and suffered thee to hunger, and fed thee with manna, which thou knewest not, neither did thy fathers know; that he might make thee know that man doth not live by bread only, but by every word that proceedeth out of the mouth of the LORD doth man live. (Deuteronomy 8:3)

God had to teach a generation of people to look to Him as their source of supply, for they had been slaves to Egypt and had known the government to be their only source of supply. It is a lesson God has to teach His children in this generation, too. *Wandering in the Wilderness*

This early passage of Scripture becomes an initial link between natural and spiritual food. God declared to them that they would live spiritually by partaking of the Word of God. He gave them manna for their bodies and divine communication for their souls.

This verse also suggests a positive side to hunger. These people did not easily adjust to change. They wanted freedom, but they complained about the absence of the food they were used to. They said:

> We remember the fish, which we did eat in Egypt freely; the cucumbers, and the melons, and the leeks, and the onions, and the garlick. (Numbers 11:5)

God let them hunger until they were willing to eat His provisions. *He lets us hunger until we yield to His will.* It was His way of creating a new set of appetite values. He often has to do this with us when our spiritual appetites have become accustomed to the flavor of the world or carnal Christianity. In this sense, God's Word portrays hunger as a positive force. Jesus said:

> Blessed are they which do hunger and thirst after righteousness: for they shall be filled. (Matthew 5:6)

Until there is a craving, few will exert the effort to be filled with righteousness. When the hunger is strong enough, any price will be paid in order to satisfy that hunger.

A tremendous spiritual hunger was created when we came to Jesus. It seemed that we could never get enough to eat. After a while, however, we got so busy with other things that we began to satisfy that craving with leftovers and spiritual junk food. Malnutrition came slowly, but our spiritual energies diminished rapidly. Like the Prodigal Son, we discovered that when we cut ourselves off from the source of supply, we eventually got seriously hungry. Hunger caused the Prodigal Son to have a serious change of mind about himself and his circumstances. We read:

> When he came to himself, he said, How many hired servants of my father's have bread enough and to spare, and I perish with hunger! I will arise and go to my father. . . . (Luke 15:17-18)

In the same tone of thought, Jesus said: "Blessed are ye that hunger now: for ye shall be filled" (Luke 6:21). He knew that hunger awakens us to our famished condition and motivates us to use our remaining strength to find food to satisfy that hunger. The blessedness of hunger is its activating power. Food-seeking is one of the strongest drives inherent in each of us. It is glorious when a Christian begins to realize that he or she is hungry, for they will begin to seek the Lord for satisfaction.

It's Me, Equipping Again

When hunger pangs begin to work in a family, the hungry ones initiate a search for something to snack on while asking, "When's dinner ready, Mom?"

Every homemaker knows that she can cook and serve only so many meals before going to the grocery store to restock the kitchen supplies. Each time she uses something, she understands it must be restocked. When the shelves of the kitchen seem bare, the wife and mother usually says, "I need to go to the store." She has confidence that there is an abundant supply of groceries available as well as an abundance of stores where these supplies can be obtained.

Those clean and well-stocked grocery shelves are no accident. During the day, hundreds of shoppers deplete the stock by transferring the merchandise from the shelves to their carts. A small army of workers busily restocks those shelves during the night in preparation for the next day's customers.

Similarly, the Christian whose life is fully stocked with the things of God has learned the secret and necessity of restocking the merchandise regularly. When a blessing is served to another, a mental note is made to restock it. When courage is shared, another supply must be obtained.

One of the great disappointments of life is to be around a person who once displayed the fruits and gifts of the Spirit, but now seems completely depleted. You feel he or she should be honest enough to hang a sign on his or her life that reads: "Out of business."

As a boy it was a tremendous treat to go to my paternal grandfather's house. He was full of the blessings of the Lord, even in his aged years. He was effervescent with the joy of the Lord, and he loved to share God's Word with everyone who came into his home. I always came away enriched.

Far too frequently to suit me, Rev. Zimmerman who was a friend of Grandpa's, would sometimes come by to visit when I was there. He may have once been filled with godliness, but as he grew older and retired from the ministry, he ceased to replenish the graces of God. He was negative, bitter and hopelessly dated. Even as a youth, I prayed that God would make me like my grandpa and preserve me from being a second Mr. Zimmerman.

Whether our lives touch thousands or reach no further than our immediate families, we need to replenish our spiritual lives regularly. When faith is used, it needs to be restocked. Mere memory of faith will not meet the day-by-day demands of life. The Bible tells us:

> So then faith cometh by hearing, and hearing by the word of God. (Romans 10:17)

If faith "cometh by hearing," it also "goeth by usage." We never get a lifetime supply of faith. We buy it by the pound or yard and use it as needed. Once used, it is gone. We need to return to the Word of God and hear God speak to our hearts in a fresh manner. Reviewing God's Word renews our faith. Fresh conversation with God brings renewed conviction of heart.

Similarly, we need to replenish our supply of hope, for we are worthless without hope. Job admitted that part of the pain of his affliction was his loss of hope. He cried:

> My days are swifter than a weaver's shuttle, and are spent without hope . . . And where is now my hope? as for my hope, who shall see it? (Job 7:6; 17:15)

In contrast to Job, David victoriously sang:

> And now, Lord, what wait I for? my hope is in thee . . . Why art thou cast down, O my soul? and why art thou disquieted within me? hope thou in God: for I shall yet praise him, who is the health of my countenance, and my God. (Psalms 39:7; 42:11)

David saw God as the source and object of his hope, and he had learned that this hope was a healing power to his soul.

Hope must be important, for the Bible mentions it 129 times in 121 separate verses. Paul saw hope as such a divine energy that he called God "the God of hope":

> Now the God of hope fill you with all joy and peace in believing, that ye may abound in hope, through the power of the Holy Ghost. (Romans 15:13)

This gives us a strong clue of how to replenish our hope. If God is the "God of hope," returning to His presence should be hope-inducing. If we "abound in hope through the power of the Holy Spirit" then the greater the flow of the Spirit through us, the greater abundance of hope we will have in the storerooms of our lives.

Situations may seem hopeless, but they are not our source of hope. When all is well, why do we need great hope? This firm expectation of all good things comes out of a fresh, vital relationship with God. We come to Him to replenish our hopes.

As surely as we need to equip ourselves again with faith and hope, we need to restock our love. These are the three abiding Christian virtues, but they are exhaustible. When love is given, it needs to be replaced. If the object of our expressed love returns love to us, we will not be depleted. Often, however, we love persons who are unwilling or unable to return love.

Life is made up of givers and takers. Loving a taker is seldom personally rewarding, but loving them is not a mistake. God commands this of Christians. Jesus said:

> But I say unto you, Love your enemies, bless them that curse you, do good to them that hate you, and pray for them which despitefully use you, and persecute you. (Matthew 5:44)

We need to realize that doing this is similar to grounding the positive pole of a battery. It quickly discharges all its stored energy. When we love the unlovely and the unloving, we must equip our lives with a fresh supply of love, for those who absorb like a sponge give us nothing in return unless squeezed firmly. John, the Apostle of love, reminded us:

> God is love; and he that dwelleth in love dwelleth in God, and God in him. (1 John 4:16)

God is the ultimate source of love, so we love one another with His inexhaustible love. When we begin to sense

9

a depletion of our love supply, we need only to return to the presence of God and draw upon His eternal source to restock our shelves.

The mature Christian has learned to go to God's storehouse regularly with a simple plea, "Lord, here I am again to restock my cupboard with faith, hope and love." His abundant supply will soon fill our shopping cart with all we can handle.

It's Me, Eating Again

One of the expressed joys following a siege of sickness is, "I'm eating again!" This is usually evidence that vital signs are near normal and the body is returning to health. Christians also should happily announce, "I'm eating again." It would show that their spiritual lives are back to normal. Jesus told the Jewish leaders of His day:

> I am the bread of life: he that cometh to me shall never hunger; and he that believeth on me shall never thirst. (John 6:35)

The heart of the message of this sixth chapter of John is that God sent His Son, Jesus, to become our life source. As we learn to be partakers of Him, we enter into the life of God.

Jesus is the only food that gives life to a person's spirit. Other things may preserve the body or enrich the soul, but Jesus alone gives life to our eternal spirits. He is our meat and drink. We must learn to be partakers of Jesus in order to maintain spiritual health and vigor. He alone is the source of our strength.

The most obvious means of feasting on Jesus is by reading the Bible with faith in our hearts. Peter said:

> Whereby are given unto us exceeding great and precious promises: that by these ye might be partakers

of the divine nature, having escaped the corruption that
is in the world through lust. (2 Peter 1:4)

The precious promises contained in the Bible become the
very food that enables us to be "partakers of the divine
nature." We do not approach the Bible as a student would
approach a textbook. We come to the Word as a hungry child
comes to the table. We come prepared to eat. We are
encouraged to enjoy the most elementary truth of God's
Word.

As newborn babes, desire the sincere milk of the
word, that ye may grow thereby. (1 Peter 2:2)

We are also encouraged to mature sufficiently enough
to be partakers of the meat of the Word. The writer to the
Hebrew Christians said:

But strong meat belongeth to them that are of full
age, even those who by reason of use have their senses
exercised to discern both good and evil. (Hebrews 5:14)

This lets us know that some can drink milk only, while
others can eat the rich, full meat of the Word. The difference
is in the level of spiritual maturity of the hungry person.
Fortunately, Jesus is sufficient for the most immature to the
most mature saint in the fellowship. God's Bible will meet
every level of spiritual need, and it will satisfy every appetite.
We simply need to get into that Book and eat and drink of
divine life.

The Bible was necessary food to us when we were first
saved. After being filled with the Holy Spirit, the Bible
became a new book to us. We fed at a higher level with the
help of the indwelling Spirit. As wonderful as that was, it
must be a continuing experience. Just as we cannot eat a huge
meal and go a week without eating again, so we cannot have

a Sunday morning serving of God's Word and survive through the week. We need to come to God's table on a daily schedule.

The greatness of past banquets does not satisfy the hunger of the present moment. This is why believers come repeatedly into the presence of the Lord and say, "It's me, eating again. I'm hungry."

It's Me, Enjoying Again

Over the sixty-plus years that I have been involved in active ministry, I have come to expect people to speak of their Bible reading and prayer time as a religious duty. They seem to delight in getting it out of the way for the day so they can get on with other things. They remind me of people who eat only to live.

Eating is more than a duty we must perform several times daily; it is a pleasure-producing activity. The appearance, aroma, texture and taste of food can be a sensuous experience. It delights our sense of sight, smell, touch, hearing and taste. Advertisers know that even a picture of food can stimulate the appetite. We are never more conscious of the number of food advertisements being aired on television than when we go on a diet. The aroma of coffee arouses us in the morning, and a piece of toast or the taste of some orange juice entices the appetite to awake from slumber and join in the joy of the day. Even the sound of frying bacon can be a sensual pleasure. God created us to enjoy dining.

This is also true of spiritual feasting. God's Word can stir every spiritual sense of the soul and spirit. Reading the Bible is more than a mental exercise. It is a spiritual delicacy that should be savored to the fullest. It will appeal to every spiritual sense we possess. It can awaken us spiritually — even more quickly than a cup of coffee awakens us naturally.

David had found the Lord to be exceedingly good, so he called for his companions to join him and:

> Taste and see that the LORD is good: blessed is the man that trusteth in him. (Psalms 34:8)

Some people approach the Bible as though it were a death sentence and not a source of life. Others view it as bitter medicine that may be good for them, but it is difficult to swallow. People with such concepts of the Bible usually spend little time in it. They have not developed an appetite for it.

The Word of God is sweet to our taste, stimulating to our souls and satisfying to our spirits. We should develop such a taste for it that we would want to feast on it whether we need the strength it offers or not. It is gratifying to commune with God in His Word.

Eating is a pleasure that is enhanced if shared with good company. It is not by accident that couples usually include the activity of sharing a meal together while on a date. The positive attitude that dining together produces is one reason why so much business is transacted during a meal. There is a level of fellowship in eating together that is not easily found anywhere else.

When we are feasting on Christ in God's Word, we share fellowship with Abraham, Isaac and Jacob. Philip, Paul and Peter are happy to dine with us and share the meat of the Word they have enjoyed. It is difficult to spend much time in the Bible without becoming aware of the fellowship of the Holy Spirit and the presence of Jesus.

How it enhances our enjoyment of a meal to sit at the table with such people. Their fellowship intensifies our enjoyment so much that we resist leaving after we have finished eating. The fellowship is almost as important as the food.

It is God's desire that His children learn to enjoy feasting on His provisions. Some of us are like the child who must be teased into eating because we have not discovered the joy of food. God takes far more pleasure in the child who sits at the table and enjoys every bite that has been provided. Eating is life-producing and it is enjoyable. The Psalmist testified:

> How sweet are thy words unto my taste! yea, sweeter
> than honey to my mouth! (Psalms 119:103)

This should be our testimony as well. When we hunger, God has provided sufficient satisfaction in His Son, Jesus, and partaking of Him is very enjoyable. But we cannot satisfy this hunger in the pigpen. We need a change of mind. We must return to the Father's house, even if that calls for sincere repentance.

2

Lord, It's Me, Repenting Again

A Change of Mind

"Robert," my mother said, "kiss Judson and make-up."

"I'd rather kiss a pig!" he responded as he turned from me.

"Then go back to your bedroom until you are willing to love your big brother," she commanded. He forfeited his supper that night, for he wasn't ready to make peace with me.

When my parents intervened in a conflict between my brothers and myself, and after the appropriate punishment was administered, the offender was forced to ask the forgiveness of the offended. In this act of repentance, two statements were required:

(1) "I'm sorry that I . . ."
(2) "I love you!"

This was to be followed with a hug and a kiss on the cheek. There were times when we would have preferred a second spanking over having to embrace and kiss our brother, but our parents were more interested in reconciled relationships than with punishment. They knew that the peace of the home demanded a loving interaction among the children and repentance opened the door for a renewed relationship.

My parents did not originate this method of restoring peace. They adapted it from the Word of God. They knew that with their authority and superior strength, they could force a change in actions, but could not force a change of attitude. They wanted their children to change their minds about their behavior.

The Bible teaches that repentance is a change of mind. In the New Testament, the word repent or repentance comes from the Greek word *metanoe* that signifies to think differently afterwards — "to reconsider." It is a change of mind that affects action. The Romans introduced this Greek word to their armed forces, and used it to command their troops to reverse the direction of their march. It was their equivalent of our "about-face!"

When God calls for us to repent, He wants an "about-face" in our thinking and behavior. True repentance demands a turning from our way to God's way, and from our attitude to His attitude.

Repentance was the second step in the return of the Prodigal Son. A severe change of circumstances brought him to poverty, and when he was hungry enough, he began to remember the full provision of his father's house. He recalled that the servants on the farm lived even better than he was living in this far off country. As he meditated on this contrast, he changed his mind about the farm, his father, and his elder brother. He determined that whether or not he would ever be received as a son again, he would at least fare better as a servant on his father's farm than he would as a son away from his father.

The sin of self-will can never be forgiven until there is a change of mind — repentance. God will not compel us to come back to His provision, but He awaits our return. To force our return would bring only a temporary change to our lives. We would go away again unless our minds were changed, and only we can change our minds.

In His foreknowledge, God knew that men and women would rebel against Him. There would come times when their own ways would seem better than God's ways. God was in a position, of course, to exert any type of punishment He desired, but His goal was to restore relationships with these whom He had created to be the objects of His love.

The sin of rebellion could not be ignored, for a peaceful home must have a central authority. Chaos, not calm, reigns where each person does his or her own thing. God had carefully explained to Adam the divine punishment for sin:

> But of the tree of the knowledge of good and evil, thou shalt not eat of it: for in the day that thou eatest thereof thou shalt surely die. (Genesis 2:17)

Death, not chastisement, is the reward sin brings. Through the prophet, God said:

> Behold, all souls are mine; as the soul of the father, so also the soul of the son is mine: the soul that sinneth, it shall die. (Ezekiel 18:4)

Repentance does not disannul this decree. Just as repentance to the offended party came *after* punishment in our home, God can honor repentance only after the penalty for violating His law has been paid.

Since the divine penalty — death — produces destruction of life as we know it, it seems to prevent repentance. Mercifully, God has provided a substitute. God demonstrated this in the Garden of Eden when He slew a lamb to make a covering for naked Adam and Eve. He further illustrated it in the sacrificial system He instituted through Moses. It was ultimately provided in the death of His own Son at Calvary. We are told:

> Christ hath redeemed us from the curse of the law, being made a curse for us: for it is written, Cursed is every one that hangeth on a tree (Galatians 3:13)

> Christ died for our sins according to the Scriptures. (1 Corinthians 15:3)

Our participation in this ultimate punishment is by personal identification. Jesus died the death we deserved — He was our substitute. Therefore, we identify with His work at the cross in declaring Christ's death to be our death, for that is what God has declared:

> Likewise reckon ye also yourselves to be dead indeed unto sin, but alive unto God through Jesus Christ our Lord (Romans 6:11).

The Greek word translated here as "reckon" is *logizomai.* It literally means "to take an inventory," that is, "to estimate or to conclude." It was a term used by bookkeepers for the debit balance or the net worth. Having considered the positives and the negatives, the *logizomai* is the result. When we compare our sin with Christ's sacrifice for that sin, we "reckon," or *logizomai* that in Christ we died; so the debt has been paid in full. The New Testament calls this identification with Christ's substitutionary death as being "saved." It declares:

> Even when we were dead in sins, hath quickened us together with Christ, (by grace ye are saved;) . . . For by grace are ye saved through faith; and that not of yourselves: it is the gift of God. (Ephesians 2:5,8)

Repenting to Restore Affiliation

Paul's personal testimony needs to be the testimony of every born-again believer:

> I am crucified with Christ: nevertheless I live; yet
> not I, but Christ liveth in me: and the life which I now
> live in the flesh I live by the faith of the Son of God,
> who loved me, and gave himself for me. (Galatians 2:20)

This apostle placed more emphasis upon a renewed affiliation than upon a punishment averted. It was not merely that the sin question had been settled in God's sight that excited Paul; he was elated that he had been restored to personal fellowship with the Almighty God.

The Bible defines repentance both broadly and narrowly. In its wider sense, repentance is:

1. An acknowledgment of sin.
2. A true sorrow for that sin.
3. An expression of desire to change from the ways of sin.

In its narrower application, repentance is a change of mind and attitude toward both sin and sinning.

The acknowledgment of sin is the first essential in being restored to fellowship with God. Such acknowledgment is difficult. As a boy, when my father faced me with the evidence and asked, "Judson, did you do this?" I found it hard to look in his face and say, "Yes, Dad, I am the one who did it." I knew that the same hand that held the evidence would shortly hold the switch. I also knew that there would be no restoration of a peaceful relationship between me and my parents until I acknowledged that I had violated the rules of the home and repented.

Now that I am an adult, I find it hard to look at the heavenly Father and say, "I did that and I am sorry." I am as quick to excuse my actions to God as I used to be to my earthly father. I might add that I am just as unsuccessful.

In the Garden of Eden, which pictures the entrance of sin

19

into the human race, God asked Adam where he was and why he was hiding from Him. Adam's reply was evasive, so God specifically asked him:

> Who told thee that thou wast naked? Hast thou eaten of the tree, whereof I commanded thee that thou shouldest not eat? (Genesis 3:11)

Rather than admit this, he blamed "the woman thou gavest me." When God asked Eve what had happened, she blamed the serpent. Neither Adam nor Eve was willing to acknowledge full responsibility for their sin. Like a wise parent, God punished all three parties to this act of disobedience.

We do not sin because of temptation. We sin because we yield to that temptation. Sin is a deliberate turning to our own way. There can be no redemption for us until we acknowledge personal responsibility for our actions. Today's generation lives in the depravity of sin because it will not acknowledge personal responsibility for its behavior to God. Our society teaches persons to blame their parents, the school system, television, or society in general for their sinning. We turn to psychologists, scholars and senators when we seek a change in our environment, when all we need to do is change our minds about sinning, and go to the Savior to obtain a change in our alignment to sin.

While placing the blame on others conveniently enables us to sidestep responsibility, it also completely prevents us from being freed from the sin. I cannot confess the sins of another, nor can I confess sins for which I accept no personal responsibility. Most of us fail to realize that in blaming others for our behavior, we give them control over our lives. The Prodigal Son did not take one step toward home until he changed his mind about himself and his condition and declared, "I will arise and go to my father" (Luke 15:18).

If our goal is to bring our lives back into affiliation with Father God, we must deal individually and personally with whatever broke that fellowship and relationship. It is rarely something of major proportion. The sins of our past were settled with Christ at Calvary. They are so forgiven that God has totally forgotten them, and they can never again interrupt our fellowship with God.

For most Christians, it is the "little" sins that break fellowship. I put the adjective little in quotes, for that is the way we view them. God views sin as sin without cataloging it. In His eyes, a little rebellion is still rebellion, and a little pride is still pride. The little sins of not praying, cheating on our tithes, murmuring, or gossiping have a way of destroying the flow of divine life that produces a harvest of grapes. These little foxes seem innocent when compared with polar bears, and they destroy our relationship with God.

Why do we consistently view repentance as a negative? The Bible pictures it as a glorious positive. It is God's approved method of starting over. Repentance enables us to forever remove a negative from our lives so we can replace it with a positive. Repentance more than tells God, "I'm wrong." It also admits, "You're right." This allows us to step from the wrong way into the right way. Produces Freedom

When children break the peace of the home with disobedience, godly parents will exert whatever pressure is necessary to bring them to repentance. Once they truly repent, peace returns. The wrong behavior is set aside and there is a change of mind about the situation. He or she enters a fresh relationship in the home. The family does not put them on probation; they are forgiven and restored to full fellowship with the family.

God is the originator of the family. When His chastening brings us to honest repentance, we are restored to full fellowship, not only with the Father, but with the rest of the family members as well.

This is why from time to time, I have had to kneel in prayer and say, "It's me again, Lord, repenting, so I can be restored to full affiliation with the Father and His children."

21

It's Me, Repenting for Actions

We are never more aware of our need for repentance than when our actions cut across the grain of God's known will. Behavior that expresses rebellion causes our consciences to signal an alarm not too unlike a fire alarm in a hotel. Every part of our being is made aware of danger, and our self-preservation instinct cries for immediate repentance. "Save yourself," is the inner cry of the heart.

If this violation is accidental or even incidental, our minds usually induce an immediate change of behavior with a verbal request for God's forgiveness. Like the wise driver who realizes he has made a wrong turn and immediately reverses his direction, a discerning Christian will do an immediate 180-degree turn when he or she is made aware that he or she has left the will of God.

I learned to fly in an area where any direction except north took me into mountainous terrain. When my instructor was teaching me to fly at night, he demonstrated to me that since the area was inhabited, I could usually find a light ahead of me. He told me that if that light should suddenly disappear, I should do an immediate 180-degree turn, for there was now something between me and that light, and it may be a mountain. It proved to be excellent advice that I heeded repeatedly. It would be judicious for Christians to do a "repentance turn" the moment the light of God's presence disappears from view, for something stands between them and God. _Whether between man & God or Men & Men._

Sometimes our disobedient actions are deliberate violations of the will of God. In these occasions, our stubbornness usually overrides the message of the mind to change course and go back. We tell ourselves that someone turned the light off and that there is nothing between us and God. Like the boater on the Niagara River, we continue to paddle our canoe downstream in spite of the roar of the waterfall. It is in such cases that we need the divine

22

intervention Paul spoke of in his letter to the church in Corinth:

> For godly sorrow worketh repentance to salvation not
> to be repented of: but the sorrow of the world worketh
> death. (2 Corinthians 7:10)

It is, obviously, far better to wrestle with divine sorrow than with destructive rebellion.

Some Christians do not seem to recognize the difference between sorrow and repentance. The purpose of sorrow is to induce repentance, but it is not, of itself, repentance. Remember that the narrower definition of repentance is "to think differently afterward." It reverses our thinking. Godly sorrow that does not induce this radical change of direction has not yet produced true repentance.

When my parents corrected and chastened me, their goal was a change in my behavior. They accepted my tears, my hugs and my declaration that I would not repeat the action, but they watched my life carefully for a season. If my behavior did not do a 180-degree change, they readministered the chastisement, for they realized that I had not truly repented. I had simply admitted my wrong because the evidence against me was overwhelming.

My heavenly Father originated this form of correction and He still implements it in my life. When His Spirit convicts me, it may reduce me to tears of remorse and expressions of sorrow that I have violated His will, but He watches to see if there is a change in my life. If not, we go back to square one!

I have found it totally impossible to defraud God. He knows my heart; so my words do not detract Him. He warns:

> Be not deceived; God is not mocked: for whatsoever
> a man soweth, that shall he also reap. (Galatians 6:7)

23

Actions determine achievement. True repentance changes both our concepts and our conduct, and it will be seen in the fruit of our lives. The godly fruit of righteousness will grow where the worldly fruit of selfishness once ripened.

When we are saved, we become "children of God" (Galatians 3:26). Although we have turned from our sinful ways, we still require much training. Paul urged us to:

> Walk in the Spirit, and ye shall not fulfil the lust of the flesh . . . If we live in the Spirit, let us also walk in the Spirit. (Galatians 5:16, 25)

The distinction between our talk and our walk is usually very evident in the first years of our Christian experience. The progressive work of the indwelling Holy Spirit is to bring our lives into complete harmony with the will of God. This calls for many course corrections in our daily walk. Each correction calls for another act of repentance that will change our direction.

This is why many of us have found ourselves coming into the presence of God on repeated occasions saying, "It's me again, Lord. I'm making another adjustment in my actions." This is positive; not negative. It leads to obedience as a replacement for disobedience. It brings us into the peace of God and replaces the confusion of being in charge of our lives. It removes our feet from the route that merely seems right to us and places them on the divine pathway.

It's Me, Repenting for Attitudes

It is self-evident that we must from time to time repent for wrong actions. That we have inordinate aspirations we must turn from is more difficult to see. We often have blind spots when it concerns wrong attitudes. It is frequently difficult to know the mood of our hearts, for the Bible says:

> The heart is deceitful above all things, and desperately wicked: who can know it? (Jeremiah 17:9)

Many of us are totally out of touch with our feelings and motives. We are far less aware of *why* we do than *what* we do. The danger here, of course, is that our attitudes affect our actions. The Word says:

> For as he thinketh in his heart, so is he. (Proverbs 23:7)

Jesus consistently placed more emphasis upon attitudes than upon actions. To Him, motivation took precedence over manifestation. He taught that it was possible to do the right thing for the wrong reason and lose our reward.

Through the years, I have found it necessary to repent regularly for improper attitudes toward myself, toward others, and toward God. I suppose this pattern will be repeated for as long as I live.

We need to realize that a wrong attitude will block the grace of God to our lives. Though He forgives us, if we do not accept that forgiveness, we live in a false sense of guilt and condemnation. Whether true or false, condemnation is limiting.

Even after honest repentance, it is possible to disbelieve God's forgiveness. Throughout the Gospels, no one ever came to Jesus to ask forgiveness whom Jesus had not already forgiven. It is still that way, for Christ's work at Calvary purchased and provided our forgiveness. Our confession of sin is merely a step into this waiting forgiveness. When Jesus spoke forgiveness, such as: "Neither do I condemn thee: go and sin no more" (John 8:11), people were released from their guilt. Those words still release guilt and restore peace to the repentant one.

I have also found it necessary to sincerely repent for my attitudes toward others. As Dr. Sam Sasser so aptly said in a recent ministerial gathering, "We all have cleat marks up our backs. Someone has used us as a bridge to somewhere." These bruises and lacerations affect our attitudes toward the person who produced them. None of us like to be used!

Learning to live with God's children produces many conflicts. We often come out of these conflicts saying all the correct religious phrases, but with incorrect real attitudes. Hugs and kisses that mask resentment and unforgiveness are overt acts of hypocrisy in the eyes of God. We need to come again to the Lord in honest repentance for these attitudes toward others — repentance that changes *our* attitudes.

As painful as it becomes, we can have wrong attitudes toward God Himself. We often hold Him responsible for extreme negatives that have happened in our lives. How often have I encountered such words as: "If God is such a good God, why did He allow my son to die?"

In praying with people, I have occasionally found them unable to talk to God because they were mad at Him. He had not answered their prayers as they prayed them (as though God were obligated to take orders from any of us), or they resented something He had done for another.

This was the problem with the elder brother in the story of the Prodigal Son. He deeply resented his father's open forgiveness of the younger son. He felt that the reception, ring, robe, repast and revelry were completely out of order. He wouldn't even participate in the celebration. This wrong attitude kept the elder brother away from:

1. **The heart's desire of the father**. The father wanted to forgive and restore the wandering son. The brother wanted penalty and separation. The elder brother couldn't love what the father loved nor did he want what the father wanted.

2. **The love of his brother**. The resentment of the elder brother kept a barrier between himself and

his younger brother. Perhaps he feared that he would now have to share the remaining portion of the inheritance with the son who had already received and squandered his portion. It prevented the younger brother from sharing his love for him.

3. **The joy of the servants.** He remained on the outside looking in rather than entering into the singing, dancing and feasting. He refused to release his anger, so he never experienced the joy.

We dare not be too critical of the elder brother, for there is some of his spirit in each of us. It is difficult for us to allow God to restore to sonship one who has turned away from God in a most despicable manner. While the Prodigal Son needed to repent of his actions to get back into fellowship with his father, the elder brother needed to repent of an improper attitude to remain in fellowship with his father.

"Lord, it's me again—repenting" should be a memorized expression in each Christian's vocabulary. It needs to be repeated almost every time we come into the presence of our heavenly Father. It is the key to forgiveness. It becomes a door into the presence of God, and it is a necessary initial step toward a change of action.

Often when I could not praise my way into God's presence, I have successfully gained entrance through repentance. As I changed my mind about God, others or myself, I found God's presence to be very real. God is more eager to have us come into His presence than we are willing to pay the price for entrance. There needs to be constant changes in us to enable us to come into the holy place with God. The beginning of those changes is repentance. "Father, forgive me, for I . . ." The next step is actually returning to Father.

3

Lord, It's Me, Returning Again

A Change of Action

"Your homework is a mess. You'll have to do it again," the teacher instructs a student.

"Our client has changed his order. This contract will have to be done over again," the boss tells an employee.

"This is the second time this week that Johnny missed the bus. You'll have to drive him to school again," a mother informs the father.

Whether we are still in the school room, in the marketplace or in the home, life hurls the word "again" at us daily. We seldom use it to describe repetitive tasks that have become habit patterns in our lives. We usually employ this word to show that something we thought was complete must be repeated.

There are times when the word "again" screams at us like bold type on a page. It says, "Repeat!" It implies failure. It stands as a barrier to progressing into new fields. All writers dread the red penciled remark, "Write this chapter again!"

"Again," is not all negative. When fall arrives and I tell my wife, "I'm going to take you to the state fair again," it evokes a very happy response, for our annual trips to the state fair have become a highlight in her life. This former farm-girl loves this "again" in her life.

Similarly, when the children ask, "Are we going to have pizza again?" it doesn't sound like a complaint. They are about to re-experience a gastronomic pleasure.

Sometimes "again" gives us another chance. Thomas Edison tried hundreds of different elements before discovering that a carbon filament in a vacuum could emit light without self-destructing when electricity flowed through it. He was willing to try his experiments again and again until he was issued a patent in 1879 for the incandescent light bulb. Success, not speed, was his goal. It was this dogged persistence that made him such a successful inventor.

"Lord, it's me again!" embraces all three of these usages of the word "again." There are times when we must come back to the Lord because of failure or because change is necessary. Sometimes, we come to the Lord again to repeat a joyful experience. Other times, "It's me again!" shows a dogged persistence of not quitting until a desired goal is reached. It always implies a returning.

It was absolutely essential that the Prodigal Son return home to survive. He was hungry and he had repented. His change of mind paved the way for a change of action, but he was still in the pigpen. It was not until his legs gave action to his new mind-set that he found himself in the presence of his father again. His life remained unchanged until he could look his father in the eyes and say, "It's me, returning from wandering."

It's Me, Returning from Wandering

It is obvious that we cannot return to a place where we have never been. The person who never had a home, cannot return home. To tell God, "It's me, returning again" is to admit that I was once in His presence.

Probably no generation of people enjoyed God more than those who came out of Egypt under the leadership of Moses. God's release, protection, provision and guidance were very personal. The Egyptians had enslaved this race of people for over 300 years. After their exodus, they experienced freedom for the first time in their lives.

God purposed far more than mere deliverance from slavery. He planned to lead them into the Promised Land and make a mighty nation out of them. Leading them into the wilderness was a process to take some of Egypt out of them, but these Israelites became quite comfortable in that wilderness. God's provision was consistent, their work load was amazingly light and the price of entering the Promised Land seemed too great to risk. When it was time to go in, they chose to stay out, and God let them have their own way. For forty years, they wandered in that barren wilderness, continuing to enjoy God's provision and protection, but lacking the joy of His presence. We read:

> But with many of them God was not well pleased: for they were overthrown in the wilderness. Now these things were our examples, to the intent we should not lust after evil things, as they also lusted. (1 Corinthians 10:5-6)

Our hearts, like theirs, are as prone to desiring our own way, even if it means wandering away from God's revealed presence. We predetermine how far we will go with God, completely forgetting that at whatever point we cease to move on with God, we lose His presence, for God doesn't halt when we stop. Choosing to wander doesn't cost us our salvation, for we are not saved by works. Paul clearly taught:

> For by grace are ye saved through faith; and that not of yourselves: it is the gift of God. Not of works, lest any man should boast. (Ephesians 2:8-9)

31

Furthermore, God mercifully continues to meet our essential needs while we wander, and He even supplies us enough rudimentary religion to satisfy our souls. This often gives us wanderers a false sense of security. We fail to distinguish the difference between God's mercy and His mission. Divine mercy prevents our complete self-destruction while we insist upon our own way, but God's unchanging mission is to bring us into something greater than we could possibly imagine. Paul reminded the sinning church at Corinth:

> Eye hath not seen, nor ear heard, neither have entered into the heart of man, the things which God hath prepared for them that love him. (1 Corinthians 2:9)

These provisions are prepared, but they will not be pushed upon us. God entices us toward them, but He will not coerce us into them. That is where He is headed, but we may choose to remain where we are.

Rejection of God's provision and our desire to remain in the status quo prevents us from entering into our inheritance, it costs us the joy of God's company, and we spend our days wandering through the same old territory. Few things in life are more boring than a religion that refuses to move into new territory with God.

Wandering is never a provision of God, though God may give provisions during our wandering. Wandering is always the result of a deliberate choice. Escape from wandering is equally a deliberate choice. Once our circumstances become unbearable and we are willing to change our minds about God's will, all we need to do is say, "Lord, it's me again, returning from my wandering." Faster than believed possible, we will be led into the beginning provisions of God's Promised Land.

One of the joys of what we loosely call "revival" is that

God's wandering people return to His presence and His higher provision. Tired of manna, water and quail, they choose to go through the Jordan into the Promised Land. In a "do or die" attitude, they walk with God into something new, and they discover how wonderful the presence of God is and how superior His provision is in His presence.

Not all who need to return merely wandered away from God. Some people genuinely lose their way. The Christian life is a totally new experience to them, and they find themselves in very different circumstances. In exploring the things that interest them, they often forget the way back to the presence of God.

Our neighbors in Yakima had a cocker spaniel that seemed to lack a homing instinct. If he meandered more than a block away, he was hopelessly lost. On occasion these neighbors would enlist the help of our mixed-breed dog to help them find their "Bing." Our "Dox" could roam for miles and still find his way back. It didn't take him long to find Bing and lead him back home.

Many Christians are like this dog Bing. They merely wander from the ways of God while exploring the ways of the world. They want to come home, but they don't know the way back. They often need someone's intervention to lead them back. Jesus asked the shepherds:

> What man of you, having an hundred sheep, if he lose one of them, doth not leave the ninety and nine in the wilderness, and go after that which is lost, until he find it? (Luke 15:4)

It's Me, Returning from Withstanding

The dog we had before Dox often chose to leave home for days at a time. Spot, as our girls called this water spaniel, was a free spirited animal. We had to keep him tied or penned

33

up or he would run away for days at a time. He eventually left us and never returned, although we repeatedly saw him around town.

Unlike those people who get disoriented and are unable to find their way back, there are many others, like our dog Spot, who rebel at the restrictions to be found in the Father's house and deliberately walk away. As the godly prophet admitted:

> All we like sheep have gone astray; we have turned every one to his own way; and the LORD hath laid on him the iniquity of us all. (Isaiah 53:6)

We sin because we turn to our own way. The answer to that sin is to turn from our own way and return to God.

Jannette is an example of this. She made a good impression. She had tastefully chosen her apparel and the accessories matched perfectly. Her hairdresser had chosen a style that emphasized her cherub-like face, and her smile would disarm almost anyone. The only blemish in this vision of loveliness was her eyes. They lacked the sparkle and joy one would expect. Instead, they reflected hurt and anxiety. "You don't remember me, do you, Brother Cornwall?" was the first thing she said to me at the front of the church after the service.

"No, dear, I'm afraid I don't," I admitted.

"I'm Jannette, the daughter of Harold and Jean Faulkner. You were their pastor about ten years ago. I am their oldest daughter — the one who used to call you Grandpa Cornwall."

"Oh, yes," I said, thankful that my memory was being stirred. "But you've certainly grown up since I last saw you."

"Up, old and worldly wise," she said as she broke eye contact with me.

When I left the church where I had pastored the Faulkners, Jannette was still in grade school. The young lady who stood before me bore little resemblance to the girl I remembered. She had the good fortune to be born to Christian parents as the oldest of three children in this middle-income family.

As Jannette again made eye contact with me, she began her story. "Although I was a good student in school and active in the church youth group, I found the rules of my parents too restrictive for me," she said. "My classmates in school seemed filled with rebellion against 'the establish-ment' and I allowed it to infect my spirit," she continued. "I consistently asserted my independence by defying almost every rule of the home. When my parents repeatedly disciplined me for this, I decided to run away from home."

I remembered having received a letter from the Faulkners asking me to join them in prayer that they could locate Jannette. For several years, it seemed as if she had disappeared off the face of the earth. Her heartbroken parents tried desperately to locate her, but she had disappeared in the depravity of New York City.

"As I look back on it," Jannette continued, "I must have been crazy. I packed a few of my clothes in Mother's suitcase and headed for the freeway. With a teasing smile, I soon caught ride after ride from Houston to New York City, but I quickly discovered that these rides were not entirely free. I was expected to 'give out' in the back seat of the car before I was allowed to leave."

"I didn't realize," she continued, "that without job skills, I couldn't find work in the city. I spent what little money I had brought with me in two days, and I found myself sleeping on a park bench. The very first night someone stole my suitcase. The third or fourth night, I was mugged for my purse."

Her story was heartbreaking. She turned to prostitution for survival and she finally became a prey to a pimp who introduced her to drugs and taught her to use her body to support her habit.

The abuse she suffered at the hands of this man staggered my imagination. What Jannette did not tell me, her mother did. When he was high on drugs, he treated her worse than most people would treat an animal. The physical and mental abuse he repeatedly poured onto her was destructive. The depravity he inflicted on her must have had demonic inspiration. She was a virtual slave of this man, and he had convinced her that she could not survive without him.

After a particularly abusive attack that became so noisy that the neighbors called the police, Jannette dared to admit to the investigating officer that she was a runaway minor and gave him the name and phone number of her parents.

"I couldn't believe how fast my parents got to me in the hospital," Jannette told me. "I was so battered that I didn't look human, but Mother threw her arms around me and wept such tears of love as to stir in me something that I hadn't felt for three years. My dear, reserved dad stood silently at the foot of the bed dropping tears onto his necktie."

"We're taking you home, darling," he said in a broken voice. "Your bedroom is just as you left it, and your sister is waiting anxiously for your return. We want you back home. The family is not complete without you."

"That's why I'm here, Brother Cornwall," Jannette said. "This is my parents' home church. I was excited when they told me you were coming. In many ways, I am starting life over. I don't know if the scars in my life will ever go away, but my parents never hold my rebellious years against me. They are giving me every possible chance to recover fully. They've offered to send me to college when I complete my high school courses."

Being a preacher, my mind quickly compared Jannette's story to the story Jesus told about the Prodigal Son. He, too, ran away from home and fell victim to wicked persons who used him until everything valuable was dissipated. When he finally left the pigpen where he was working and returned home to his father, he, too, was received with open arms and was restored to his position in the home.

One of the great positives of God's Word is that He always welcomes home a runaway son or daughter. For many years, I heard impassioned sermons on how difficult it was for a "backslider," as we designated Christian runaways in those days, to return to the Lord. If there is difficulty, it is with the floater, not with the Father. The problem, if it exists, is with personal pride, not with parental prohibition. No person who has rebelled against the rules of the Father's house needs to fear rejection upon returning. The promise of Jesus is:

> All that the Father giveth me shall come to me; and him that cometh to me I will in no wise cast out. (John 6:37)

This is both inclusive and conclusive. None is excepted; all are accepted.

Reception and restoration are God's consistent responses to our repentance. The rebel need say little more than, "Lord, it's me again, returning from withstanding Your ways." He or she will find the robe, the ring, the kiss and the fatted calf awaiting their return. Turning to our own way does not mean automatic expulsion from the family of God. It does, however, mean privation, pain and self-inflicted penalty. Fortunately, the work of Christ on the cross can undo the work of rebellion and redo the work of redemption in our lives.

It's Me, Returning from My Ministry

We frequently find it difficult to want what God desires for us. Like self-willed children, we prefer our dreams to the wisdom of our parents. We all have personal ambitions, physical desires and private fantasies in our lives. We often transport these into our Christian experiences and seek to make spiritual entities of them. The giftings and the callings of God often enable us to build personal kingdoms and inflated reputations in the church world where the competition is less fierce than in the commercial world.

We are too familiar with Christian artists who have used the Christian platform to establish their reputation as performers. What begins as "a ministry unto the Lord" often degenerates into using the Lord to create performers who build their egos with applause and their financial portfolios through ticket and tape sales.

We have seen similar patterns of behavior in gifted speakers. They, too, may have begun their ministry desiring to benefit the Body of Christ, but their personal aspirations overtook their initial dedication, and they motivated the Christians into benefiting them. Many anointed ministers feel they cannot minister without forming a foundation that bears their individual names. If this is God's will for them, all is well. Unfortunately, many times this is simply the personal ambitions of these individuals. Raising money to support the foundation quickly replaces sharing the ministry God had imparted to them.

I have observed through my sixty years of ministry that few things are more difficult than remaining in the arena of God's calling. Our American philosophy continues to press us to expand into other fields, or to enlarge our ministries beyond the scope of God's divine anointing. Ambition drives us beyond our abilities, and our competitive natures cause us to attempt whatever is succeeding for others.

Ambition is not wrong. We are worthless without it, but ambition goes wrong when our natural aspirations move us out of the will of God. Any time ambition replaces God's anointing, we have sinned and need to repent.

I have often seen cattle standing in a lush pasture straining to reach over the fence for a mouthful of grass. I have watched them take repeated jolts from an electric fence just to eat what seems to be forbidden food. In reality, the food those cows were standing in was the same as what was growing over the fence.

Like cattle, we, too, have seasons when we feel that the grass on the other side of the fence is greener than on our side. Apparently we view God as a tease or one Who delights in giving us second best, for no matter what He has given to us, it appears that what He gave to another is better and we want it.

A few years ago, I was invited to minister at a large church in a southern city. The first night of the conference, the pastor announced his candidacy for the United States Senate. The people cheered and applauded, but I felt heart-sick.

The following day I spoke briefly with this pastor. I reviewed for him how he had come to this city and gathered a great congregation of people. He had successfully led them in constructing a beautiful edifice to accommodate them. I told him that this was God's calling and sphere of anointing for him. I reminded him that Charles Spurgeon told his ministerial students, "If God has called you to preach the Gospel, never stoop to becoming the Prime Minister of England."

My words were rejected. He felt confident of victory and was convinced that he could make a significant change in our congress. Perhaps in the mercy of God, the voters decisively rejected him. A later attempt to secure a seat in the state senate equally failed. After the second defeat, he was open to counsel and reentered the ministry. When he returned to God's original calling upon his life, he again became a successful pastor. His only scars were great indebtedness and wasted years.

When our aspirations violate God's aim for our lives, we need to repent and change our actions. Even if we could succeed in fulfilling our dreams, we will have failed in the eyes of God. Through Samuel, God told Israel's first king, Saul:

> Hath the LORD as great delight in burnt offerings
> and sacrifices, as in obeying the voice of the LORD?
> Behold, to obey is better than sacrifice, and to hearken
> than the fat of rams. (1 Samuel 15:22)

It is amazing what dedication, talent, sacrifice and application can do to fulfil our desires, but if they are not harmonious with the callings of God, they will end up as ashes in the day of final testing.

God is completely unimpressed with what we can do for Him. He desires for us to discover what He can do through us. He is not looking so much for ability as availability. He used many people in the Bible who lacked native competence, but they presented innate obedience. The Bible never pronounces a blessing upon a person's genius, but it does declare:

> O LORD of hosts, blessed is the man that trusteth
> in thee. (Psalms 84:12)

It is not talent, but trust that God seeks to find in men and women. His proficiency more than compensates for our inadequacy. He simply says: "Trust Me!"

God knows what He is doing, why He is doing it, and how we fit into that program. He would prefer to have us work *with* Him than *for* Him. Our independent initiative hinders the work of the Lord far more than it helps. We are people under orders, not people who are giving Him orders. He consistently considers Himself the Shepherd of the sheep. He leads; we follow. He speaks; we listen.

We can read or talk this far easier than we can live it. Submission to the revealed will of God usually seems self-limiting. This innate desire to improve on God's will puts our lives in opposition to God very much as Lucifer did in heaven. His was a five-fold expression of "I will" (see Isaiah 14). The example of Jesus in the Garden of Gethsemane just before His crucifixion needs to be emulated by each of us. We read:

> And he said, Abba, Father, all things [are] possible unto thee; take away this cup from me: nevertheless not what I will, but what thou wilt. (Mark 14:36)

No matter how bitter we may perceive God's prepared cup to be, His will always produces sweet results.

The Prodigal Son faced the bitter possibility that he would be reduced to servant level if he returned home, but he had convinced himself that this was preferable to eating the husks that he fed to the swine. His hunger produced repentance, and once he sincerely changed his mind, he returned home with a prepared speech asking for forgiveness. Jesus does not indicate that the speech was ever given, for the father's hugs and kisses prevented any conversation. It satisfied the father that his youngest son had changed his mind sufficiently to change his actions. It was not the son's words, but his action that excited the father.

Only eternity will reveal how often I have had to lift my voice to my heavenly Father and cry: "Lord, it's me, returning again." I doubt if my words are as meaningful to God as my change of mind and actions.

After my return to the center of God's will, I wonder why it took me so long to admit that my way was wrong. I am usually greatly ashamed of my past actions, attitudes and aspirations, but my Father has a wonderful way of overriding shame.

4

Lord, It's Me, Ashamed Again

A Change of Attitude

A well-told story doesn't bore the listener with all the details. Jesus was a master story teller who could condense the related incident to its salient points without telling everything that happened. The story of the Prodigal Son is a beautiful case in point. We are told everything necessary to understand the story and make the application, but many details are left untold.

Our imaginations can very well supply anything that Jesus did not say. It is to be expected that as the Prodigal Son got closer to his home territory, his sense of shame almost became overwhelming. He probably paused at a drainage ditch and gave himself the best bath possible. He may have washed his clothes and wrapped them around himself in such a way as to conceal tears and stains.

He had left home as a favored son. Now he was returning in defeat and disgrace. The shame in his heart showed on his face. When the father ran toward him, the son couldn't even look him in the eyes. This son was amazed to be recognized in his tattered condition, and he was ashamed to admit who he was.

When we return to Jesus after a season of wandering, we often discover that our greatest pain is personal shame. *The Merriam Webster's Seventh New Collegiate Dictionary* defines shame as:

> A painful emotion caused by consciousness of guilt, shortcoming, or impropriety — the susceptibility to such emotion — dishonor, disgrace — something that brings strong regret.

Shame is an emotion each of us has experienced, but it is not an emotion that God wants us to live in or under. He has exhorted us in His Word:

> Study to shew thyself approved unto God, a workman that needeth not to be ashamed, rightly dividing the word of truth. (2 Timothy 2:15)

The Greek word the King James Version translates as *study* is *spoudazo* which means to make an effort — to be diligent — to endeavor. The *Revised Standard Version* more accurately translates this verse: "Do your best to present yourself to God as one approved, a workman who has no need to be ashamed." What we are is more important to God than what we do, and, whether we realize it or not, it is to us as well. The Apostle John shared a similar message with the believers when he wrote:

> And now, little children, abide in him; that, when he shall appear, we may have confidence, and not be ashamed before him at his coming. (1 John 2:28)

Other New Testament writers assure us that we need not be ashamed, but practical Christian living proves that we are ashamed far too frequently. Shame and guilt function much as a hand and glove. They were made for each other. When

44

the hand of guilt is laid aside, the glove of shame should also go. Unfortunately, some Christians keep useless gloves in the closet of their memories.

Shame is not a by-product of embracing Bible principles as a life-style. Shame is inherent to our human natures, for all cultures of the world reflect shame, and all religions seek to deal with it. The Bible is not a producer of shame; neither does it ignore shame. It mentions *shame* 100 times in 98 separate Scripture verses and uses the word *ashamed* 122 times in 111 verses. God's Book helps to pinpoint the cause of shame and offers us a way out of our shame.

Shame is a painful emotion that destroys a healthy self-image and restricts positive participation in a joyful Christian experience. Some people retreat from participating in life when overwhelmed with shame, but Christians who have a talking relationship with Jesus come before Him to admit, "Lord, it's me, ashamed again."

It's Me, Ashamed of the Things I've Not Done

The Prodigal Son had to wrestle with shame over things left undone. He had not contacted anyone at home since he left. He had not invested wisely. He had not followed through with the work ethic his father had taught him. He had not held to his religious training, or he would never be feeding pigs. He had to handle this shame and change his attitude or he could never have come home to the farm.

There are times when we have valid reasons for being ashamed of the things we've not done. How many have come to Jesus very late in life and are ashamed of the wasted years. Others of us are genuinely ashamed of not having obeyed the Lord in specific areas of our lives. Sometimes, to our shame, we fail to keep covenants made with one another, and the way many Christians handle their finances is shameful.

When we look back over our shoulders, aren't we

ashamed of not having helped others? We saw the need, but were too busy or preoccupied to say the kind word, pray the strengthening prayer, or write the needed check. Our conscience hurt for a few minutes, but we repressed the feeling and got on with our lives. Like all repressed feelings, this regret occasionally rises and joins with similar remorse; causing us to be ashamed of our self-centeredness in the face of others' needs.

We dare not shrug off these things we've not done. We need to allow the cry of our conscience to produce a change in our behavior. The shame of past neglect can become a prod to motivate us to present involvement. As long as we are alive we are capable of adjustment and change. We can come to Jesus and say, "I'm ashamed of what I have not done. Please get me moving again!"

There are times when we compare our accomplishments with what others have done and we say, "I'm ashamed of myself for doing so little." God does not assign the same responsibilities to all. His giftings become His enablings, but He doesn't give equal gifts to us all.

When I taught the organ, I discovered that having a desire to play this instrument wasn't the entire secret to success. There is a need for a musical ability. Those who possess it move easily onto the keyboard, while those who do not possess it struggle with the mechanics of music and succeed only in sounding a bit like a player piano — they may be technically accurate, but there is no feeling or flow in the music.

The person who lacks musical skills is often very gifted in other ways. Rather than be ashamed of what they can't do, they should major on and be thankful for the personal skills they do have.

While it is the time for honest confession, we might as well admit that we feel ashamed at having been hurt just as much as we are ashamed for hurting others. We have been told for years that it is not what happens to us that hurts us, but how we react to that happening. When we read in the Bible of the suffering some people endured for their testimony of Jesus, it makes us ashamed of our weak endurance. The writer of the Book of Hebrews sums up much of this by saying:

> Women received their dead raised to life again: and others were tortured, not accepting deliverance; that they might obtain a better resurrection: And others had trial of cruel mockings and scourgings, yea, moreover of bonds and imprisonment: They were stoned, they were sawn asunder, were tempted, were slain with the sword: they wandered about in sheepskins and goatskins; being destitute, afflicted, tormented; (Of whom the world was not worthy:) they wandered in deserts, and in mountains, and in dens and caves of the earth. And these all, having obtained a good report through faith, received not the promise. (Hebrews 11:35-39)

They suffered in faith while we have suffered in fear. It makes us ashamed of ourselves. Perhaps twentieth-century living has made us too soft or maybe personal well-being has replaced our perception of the will of God. Modern Christians seem more body-oriented than spirit-conscious. We seem more interested in being healthy than in being holy.

Sometimes the shame we carry is projected upon us. Many, if not all of us, were repeatedly told during our childhood, "Shame on you!" Until that moment, we felt no shame for our behavior, but we accepted the projected guilt because it came from an authority figure. It established a pattern of accepting projected shame whether we are guilty or not. We've come to believe that if others feel we should be ashamed, we should accommodate them. Because of this, many of us have seasons of being conscience-stricken even though we are guiltless.

Some people are ashamed of the way they look or of their limited education because others have told them, "You ought to be ashamed of yourself." In spite of the Preamble to the United States Constitution, all men (or women) are not created equal. There is no reason to be ashamed of the body that we were born with or to be ashamed of the family into which we were born. What we have done with our life is far more important than what we look like or our family origin.

A noted evangelist expressed shock to me a few years ago when he discovered that I drove a Ford and wore J. C. Penney suits.

"A man of your position in the Body of Christ should be ashamed to live that way," he told me. "You are a poor representative of Jesus!"

Perhaps he had forgotten that Jesus wore homemade clothes and usually traveled by foot. The only time he rode was on a donkey. Even a Ford Mustang is better than a donkey!

To have accepted the projected shame from this evangelist would have made me unduly self-conscious and may well have depleted my bank account in my effort to live up to his standard of living. This was his problem, not mine.

We need to take a good look at the person who projects shame onto others. We also need to decide whether the projected guilt pertains to our lives or not. To shoulder blame every time someone projects it is to allow them to control our lives.

It's Me, Ashamed of Things I've Done

Inactivity and inattention to the will of God are not the only reasons for our shame. Whenever I look at hurting people, I'm ashamed of the hurts I have inflicted on others — especially of the hurts I have imposed upon members of the Body of Christ. Not all my words have been gracious and kind. Not all my counsel has been correct. Because my wife loves me so devotedly, she is especially vulnerable to me, and the deepest wounds she has received, I have inflicted.

I am not proud of any of this. I am ashamed. I wish God had a time machine that would allow me to go back to certain situations and seasons of my life. If I could take my present knowledge with me, I would do many things differently. But I cannot go back, and beyond asking forgiveness from the people I have hurt, I cannot undo the damage I have caused. All I can do now is learn to handle the shame that would rob me of a victorious walk in God.

It is my guess that if you were writing instead of reading this book, you could say what I have just said. All of us have areas in our past that project shame to us. Only a perfect man has lived without hurting another, and the only perfect men we ever hear of are the dear, departed husbands of widowed wives.

We are not merely ashamed of having hurt others, but we are often deeply chagrined over our past performances. Few of us could pass the Senate hearings for a federal judgeship. We have behavior in our pasts that God has forgiven and cleansed, but we don't want it openly displayed before the public. Every memory of it brings a fresh sense of shame.

If ever a man has had a dynamic confrontation with God that was life-changing, it was the Apostle Paul on the road to Damascus. This self-willed religious zealot became a God-controlled saint with apostolic authority, and his life and ministry has touched millions of people. Still, for all his divine revelations and success in pioneering the Gospel in Asia, Paul never forgot his early misdeeds. He wrote:

> This is a faithful saying, and worthy of all accep-
> tation, that Christ Jesus came into the world to save
> sinners; of whom I am chief. (1 Timothy 1:15)

That Paul did not use the past tense and say "I *was* chief," suggests that when he reflected on his past behavior, he was still ashamed of the things he had done. He was human. It is we who have conferred sainthood upon him.

Like Paul, we, too, carry personal guilt long after Christ has pardoned us from all sin. When reminded of the life we lived before our conversion, we frequently say, "I'm so ashamed of myself!"

True honesty will cause us to admit that many things have happened since our conversion that have induced deserved, genuine shame. Statisticians declare that if Christians actually paid into their churches what they claim on their income taxes, few churches would have financial trouble. We should be ashamed of ourselves in this behavior.

Mistreatment of pastors, church splits over non-issues, and pastoral use of the pulpit to flog the sheep are all bases for being ashamed. Sexual misconduct, frivolous divorce, and child abuse should make Christians so ashamed that they cry out to God for His forgiveness as they pray: "Lord, it's me hurting with shame again. Forgive me, and help me to restructure my life."

It's Me, Ashamed of Family Members

A third area that produces shame in us is the behavior of family members. There is a bonding in a large family that makes each member feel responsible for the action of other members. The Bible requires this interaction of Christians. Paul wrote:

> Rejoice with those who rejoice, and weep with those who weep. Be of the same mind toward one another. Do not set your mind on high things, but associate with the humble. Do not be wise in your own opinion. (Romans 12:15-16, NKJ)

This command refuses to allow us to be selective in our associations in the Body of Christ, and this can prove to be embarrassing, for not all people are as great and gracious as we are. Even the way some Christians worship God can embarrass us, and their application of God's Word to everyday life mortifies us.

When we see such a wholesale turning from the Word of the Lord in many Christian circles today, we cannot help being ashamed of these family members. The press has openly revealed sins of a shocking nature among some very visible clergy in America. Some are in prison for misappropriation of funds, and others have been defrocked for sexual immorality. Priests, pastors and teachers of Christian schools have been hailed into court for sexual abuse of children.

Because there is no longer any place to hide, the public has been made aware that some preachers who cry loudly for funds do not use them as designated. Some have pled for missionary offerings without admitting that they consider themselves the missionary and their children the heathen. Some of these people of God live in great luxury while taking welfare checks from sensitive Christians and have no remorse for doing so.

None of this has escaped the television and newspaper reporters. It makes sensational copy and creates great viewer or reader interest. Unfortunately, it tends to tar all ministers and teachers with the same brush. While the non-Christians may delight in reading of such misconduct, those of us who love the Lord and seek to walk in integrity are terribly ashamed of those who have been revealed as living in sin.

I openly wept after hearing on the radio that a nationally known evangelist had again been caught in the sin he had so publicly repented of earlier. I was ashamed and my shame hurt me deeply. I hurt for myself, but I also hurt for many hundreds of people who have been damaged by this action.

51

Our shame is not only in the leaders of Christianity in our nation. We equally have reason to be ashamed of the serious lack of spiritual life in most American churches and of the powerlessness of many of God's people. It is getting more and more difficult to tell the difference between a Christian and a non-Christian. They seem to have the same life-styles, same ambitions and same passion for possessions.

Like families that have hidden a seriously retarded family member in shame, we often wish we could lock some Christians in a back bedroom and hide them permanently. We are ashamed of the way they misuse the Gospel and prostitute the power of God. We are embarrassed that the powerful Gospel has not been allowed to effect a transformation in the lives of those who attend our churches. They carry the name of God, but they are seriously retarded in the nature of God.

We can moralize that we are not responsible for their actions, and we can use their conduct as a warning for us to walk in integrity and honesty before our God. But this does not lessen the pain of our hurt. We need to come to God again with the honest confession, "Lord, it's me, hurting again because of my forced association with other family members." If we don't get help in removing this shame, we may well withdraw ourselves from the family of God. Thousands have done this, but few of them have maintained a spiritual life in their isolation. Sheep need the flock for survival. When we withdraw from other believers because we are ashamed of the behavior of a few, we often take on the spirit of an elder brother. We live in the pain of the younger brother's way of life, and in pride that we are not like him. Sometimes our dignity becomes more sinful than the brother's degradation.

The elder brother in Christ's story of the Prodigal Son was ashamed of the way the Prodigal Son had lived. When he returned home, this elder brother would not even participate in the welcome home party the father threw for the Prodigal Son. All he could do was complain and rehash the deeds of his brother. This son had apparently withdrawn into himself during the years when his brother was away from the farm, and had not found healing for the shame that came to him. One wonders if the shame over his brother had separated him from a close relationship with the father, for the father didn't even send for the elder brother to come to the banquet. He found out about it because of the noise created by the party. Rather than ask his father to forgive the shame he had because of his brother, he complained that the prodigal had returned to a welcome. It is easy for us to maintain the same spirit toward those who cause us to suffer shame.

It's Me, Ashamed of Being Ashamed

There was a time when our shame was constructive in our lives, for it was part of the motivation behind our coming to Jesus. We learned that Christ bore our guilt and our shame for us at Calvary. We confessed our sins and imputed them to Jesus. With grace and mercy beyond our wildest expectations, He paid the complete penalty for those sins and forgave us unconditionally. We released our guilt, embraced His forgiveness, but often held onto our shame. Too frequently we share with David when he sang:

> My confusion is continually before me, and the shame of my face hath covered me. (Psalms 44:15)

It is difficult, if not impossible, to live a productive life when we are covered with shame. We need God's help to let the shame of our behavior go to the cross along with the sin that caused the shame. There is an entirely new life awaiting us on the other side of the resurrection, but resurrection requires a preceding death.

Joel wrote a short prophetic book in the Old Testament

in which he predicted the ruin and restoration of the nation Israel. Peter quoted Joel's prophecy and declared: "This is that which was spoken by the prophet Joel" (Acts 2:16). Because of this association, we dare to view the book of Joel as prophetic of the New Testament Church that was born on the Day of Pentecost.

Twice in this short prophetic book, God declares that: "My people shall never be ashamed" (verses 26-27).

If we take this statement out of context, the verses are untrue, for there is much in today's Church of which we are ashamed. We, the Church, and we as individuals, should be and are ashamed of things we've not done, things we've done and of things some family members have done. There is no need playing games with God or with ourselves. We frequently need to come to God to say, "It's me, ashamed again."

Still, God says: "My people shall not be ashamed." This is not only the message of God through the prophet Joel, it is equally the message of God through the Apostle Paul. He wrote:

> For the scripture saith, Whosoever believeth on him shall not be ashamed. (Romans 10:11)

If God says we will not be ashamed, He must have made provision to release us from shame. That is the dominant message of the New Testament, and it is also found in the Old Testament.

The repeated promise in Joel is in a context of divine restoration and has preceding provisions attached:

> Ye shall eat in plenty, and be satisfied, and praise the name of the LORD your God, that hath dealt wondrously with you: and my people shall never be ashamed. . . . And ye shall know that I am in the midst

> of Israel, and that I am the LORD your God, and none
> else: and my people shall never be ashamed. (Joel 2:26-27)

The first condition, which is also a provision, is that we will be satisfactorily filled with nourishment. The New Testament application is that we will find all the spiritual food we need in God's Word. When shame weakens our faith and courage, we need to return to the source of strength God has provided in the Bible.

The second condition is praising the name of the Lord. When we turn from condemning ourselves for shameful actions or from criticizing others for making us ashamed of them, to praising the Lord, all sense of shame is dissipated, for there is nothing in the Lord that is shame-producing. Praise lifts our consciousness from self to the Savior and turns us from recrimination to rejoicing.

The third prerequisite is knowing that God is in our midst. It is when God's people recognize His presence among them and acknowledge that He has a complete monopoly as LORD that we cease to be ashamed. We begin to realize we are His people, and that it is His Church. The needed changes are His responsibility and not ours.

It is the work of the indwelling Holy Spirit, in harmony with the written Word of God, that brings us out of our shame and back into a rejoicing relationship with the Lord. The Word declares God's provision for our lives and the Holy Spirit applies that provision to daily behavior.

Our behavior triggers guilt in our consciences that screams *rejection*. The Bible, illuminated by the Spirit, whispers *acceptance*. We slowly come to realize that God doesn't expect absolute perfection from us, but He has chosen to live in our hearts to bring us to progressive perfection. We may be ashamed of where we are in our maturity, but He understands the process and He knows what we will become under His guidance. While we may expect God to be as

55

ashamed of us as we are of ourselves and of one another, He has assured us:

> For both he that sanctifieth and they who are sanctified are all of one: for which cause he is not ashamed to call them brethren. (Hebrews 2:11)

Just as we are unashamed of baby behavior in an infant, so God is unashamed of our immaturity, for He knows we will grow and develop in His holiness. If He is not ashamed of us in our baby state, perhaps we should be less ashamed and give more praise that He is our proud Father.

Perhaps we need to come into His presence and pray, "Lord, it's me again; ashamed of myself and of others. Please help me to see myself and them as You see them. As You have cleansed my guilt, help me to release my shame and change my attitude so I may enjoy You as You say You enjoy me, and this will help me to get through my hurting. Amen!"

3-30-96
Shame
about passed

5

Lord, It's Me, Hurting Again

A Change of Condition

When the Prodigal Son returned home, he was far more than hungry and ashamed. He was hurting. It is likely that he had built a defensive wall around himself for self-preservation, but when he saw the familiar property and was welcomed so warmly by his father, that wall crumbled and exposed the pain and deep wounds that had accumulated over the years. Disappointments, broken promises, failed relationships and fickle friends had hurt him deeply.

More than his pride was wounded. He hurt from misplaced trust that had been repeatedly violated. His ego which had been inflated by friends appreciating his wealth was completely deflated by having to care for pigs. He had misplaced his love in people who only liked him for his possessions.

All of us fit in one or more of these categories. Life is fragile and we are easily wounded. Some of us are more aware of these wounds than others. It is difficult to be aware of hurting when God's love is present, however. The flow of divine love seems to numb us like a local anesthetic, but this does not immunize us from wounds. Wounds will come.

It is only later that the pain of the inflicted wound can be felt.

We are acquainted with hurts and hurting, for this is what initially brought us to Jesus. Many of us were so wounded emotionally, spiritually and even physically that Christ was our last resort. If He didn't heal us, we would die. Our testimony is that He did heal us.

As the healing love of Jesus flowed into our lives, we were able to rebuild broken relationships, respond to life more maturely, and regain our physical strength. It was glorious to discover that redemption was also regeneration, and that Christ was making all things new for us.

In some ways, our conversion experience was like a seed taken out of a packet and placed in the warm, moist earth. Life began to spring forth as growth replaced dormancy. Our purpose for being was slowly released until others could see the plant that was already in the seed.

The nail-scarred hands of love that planted us in God's prepared field were gentle and caring. We felt so secure in those hands that we were convinced that nothing could ever hurt us again, but we were wrong. While the enemy of the seed could no longer get to us, we soon discovered that there are enemies. By experience we understood what Solomon meant when he spoke of:

> The foxes, the little foxes, that spoil the vines: for
> our vines have tender grapes. (Song of Solomon 2:15)

As we grew and developed in God's great love, we learned that there are individuals in His kingdom who specialize in nipping new growth with their mouths. There are others who seek to root us out of the soil with their paws. All this is pain-producing. It is not the same hurt that sin had produced in us, but it hurts. Part of the depth of the hurt is the total unexpectedness of it. We thought that the Christian family would be perfect. We trusted and loved our brothers and sisters in Christ, never dreaming that this very action made us extremely vulnerable to their woundings.

While being in the flock of God offers us some protection, that same flock may become the source of our wounds. Other sheep can stomp on us, shut us out of the circle or deprive us of needed food. This is when we need to get to the Great Shepherd of the sheep and cry, "It's me, hurting again."

Jesus, who declared Himself to be our Great Shepherd, can relate to our hurts, for He, too, was hurt by the very people He came to earth to help. The prophet Zechariah foresaw this and wrote:

> And one shall say unto him, What are these wounds in thine hands? Then he shall answer, Those with which I was wounded in the house of my friends. (Zechariah 13:6)

Our Lord experienced most of the hurts that plague our lives. He survived temptation that attacked His divine nature. Satan repeatedly said, "If thou be the Son of God . . . ," and then tried to get Jesus to prove who He was by using spiritual power for personal gain. Jesus knows the pain we feel when our position in Christ is challenged and we have no answer other than our faith.

Jesus knew ridicule, too, for when Philip sought Nathanael to tell him about the Messiah, Nathanael replied with a rather popular saying:

> Can there any good thing come out of Nazareth? Philip saith unto him, Come and see. (John 1:46)

Our Lord also faced false accusations. His authority over demons became threatening to the religious leaders of the day—threatening because they couldn't do what Jesus did:

> The scribes which came down from Jerusalem said,
> He hath Beelzebub, and by the prince of the devils
> casteth he out devils. (Mark 3:22)

It does not prevent us from hurting to know that He hurt while here on earth, but it does help us understand that He knows what we are going through, and that He is available to help us in the midst of our suffering.

It's Me, Hurting from Abuse

The word *abuse* is currently getting great notice in the press. People from all walks of life are reporting abuse that they experienced in their pasts — especially during their childhood years. They tell us of beatings, isolation, starvation and sexual molestation while they were too young to defend themselves. These experiences have left more than emotional scars; they have left wounds that seem to refuse to heal.

Christians, too, have known abuse. For some it was the pain of these memories that brought them to Jesus. Others lived fragmented lives because of abuse and the results of this fragmentation brought them to Christ. Jesus recognized that it was the distressed people who came to Him. When asked about this:

> Jesus answering said unto them, They that are whole
> need not a physician; but they that are sick. (Luke 5:31)

For many, coming to Christ did not end the physical abuse they had suffered for years. Among the faithful worshipers in our churches is a sprinkling of battered wives. They cover their bruises with make-up and put on a big smile, but inwardly they are hurting. Sometimes the abusing husband is an officer in the church, and his wife does not want to expose this side of his nature to the congregation.

Most Sunday school teachers have noticed suspicious bruises and wounds on the bodies of their students. Often these physical abuses come from an authority figure in the home who is not a Christian. Sometimes, however, even Christian parents lose control of their emotions and inflict abuse on family members. It is difficult to talk to these children about the loving heavenly Father right after their earthly father has sexually or physically abused them. Their concept of an authority figure is seriously distorted and they are hurting.

Physical abuse creates pain that goes far beyond the body. Wounds heal and bruises go away, but the deep inner pain remains in the soul. This pain often forms a barrier that makes loving contact with God very difficult.

During the years when I pastored, I used to watch the people of my congregation during worship sessions. Those who could not join us in open praise and worship of Jesus were usually those who had been abused by an authority figure in their past. Until we could help them heal these wounds, we could not bring them into a worship experience.

Physical abuse is not foreign to the Christian experience. Even Christ experienced violent physical abuse, for before His crucifixion, the Roman soldiers beat him with rods, blindfolded and repeatedly hit Him with their fists while challenging Him to prophesy who it was that hit Him. They plucked out His beard by the roots, and put a crown of poisonous thorns on His brow as they battered Him over the head with a rod. He was so abused that the prophet Isaiah claimed that on His way to the cross, He didn't even look like a man.

Jesus deserved none of this abuse, but He suffered vicariously for us. Enduring those things that wound us not only made Him an understanding High Priest, but they also made Him an approachable Savior when we are hurting. We read:

> For we have not an high priest which cannot be touched with the feeling of our infirmities; but was in all points tempted like as we are, yet without sin. (Hebrews 4:1)

More damaging than physical abuse is the sexual abuse inflicted by parents upon their children. It is unfortunate that statistics of such abuse in America show that it is even prevalent among professing Christians. In my travels to other nations, pastors report to me that such abuse is even more prevalent in their lands than in America. It is shameful that adults are willing to sacrifice the mental and emotional stability of their children just to satisfy a distorted sex drive. It is more than shameful. It is tragic when Christian believers, who have the power of the indwelling Spirit of God, allow their animal natures to control them at such a price.

Even reaching adulthood does not guarantee protection from sexual abuse. Many women have testified to the seduction and imposition of the spiritual authority of pastors that caused them to submit to his (or her) sexual advances. Because the minister represents God, he (or she) is viewed as an authority figure who is equal to the father or mother in the home. No matter how it is approached, these sexual liaisons between preacher and parishioner produce deep wounds that prevent further progress in the Christian experience.

As serious as physical and sexual abuse is, it does not fully represent all the abuse that Christians suffer. There is also the relational abuse where someone takes undue advantage of our filial relationships. I well remember the pain I suffered when a Christian publisher repeatedly pressed me to write a book on a specific subject. Although the book went into multiple printings, I was never paid any royalties. This publisher sold the publication rights to this book to another publisher who sold several printings of the book without paying me anything. It was all done in the name of God, and I was told that my writing was a "ministry." The truth was that they stole money that in all rights belonged to me. They were abusing me in the name of Christian family relationships. It was not merely the loss of needed funds that hurt me as much as I felt betrayed and emotionally raped by them.

During my lifetime of ministry, some of the most difficult counseling I have done has been with people who have been hurt by fellow Christians. Once I tried to console a precious Christian who lost his life's savings by investing them in a "Christian project" that failed. With the advantage of hindsight, he realized that it was doomed to failure from the beginning. He admitted that he made very little inquiry into the project before investing. "He is a Christian brother and I trusted him," he said. Unfortunately, this trusted one's salvation experience did not make him a good businessman, nor did it prevent him from taking undue advantage of his Christian family relationships. After such experiences, it is easy to join in David's anger and say:

> Let them be confounded and put to shame that seek
> after my soul: let them be turned back and brought to
> confusion that devise my hurt. (Psalms 35:4)

All losses are painful, but breach of trust compounds the pain. We desperately need to learn to come to Jesus with each fresh hurt and pray, "Lord, it's me, hurting again." He cannot only sympathize; He can take away the pain.

It's Me, Hurting from Rejection

Open confrontation is easier to take than private rejection. Most of us would prefer to be challenged than to be ignored. Jesus understands the pain of rejection from personal experience. Some people were determined to reject Him from the very day of His birth. In the prologue to his gospel, the Apostle John said of Jesus:

He came unto his own, and his own received him not. But as many as received him, to them gave he power to become the sons of God, even to them that believe on his name. (John 1:11-12)

Christians who have undergone the pain of divorce live with severe feelings of rejection, especially if they were exchanged by their mates for another partner. My wife's youngest sister suffered much abuse from her husband. Over the years, he was grossly and openly unfaithful to her, but she felt it was her Christian duty to remain as his wife. Eventually he broke up another marriage, divorced his wife and married the other man's wife. This ultimate rejection almost destroyed my sister-in-law, but an even deeper hurt came when she was relieved as the church organist because she was divorced. She and her children were pushed out of every activity in the church and treated as though they had "spiritual AIDS." Those wounds have never completely healed, especially in the now-grown children.

Many children of single parents live with a feeling of having been rejected by the departing parent. This pain is very real, and it has a noticeable effect upon the way these children relate to life around them. It is strong negative input into their self-image.

When we accepted Jesus as our Savior, many of us experienced immediate rejection as former friends walked out of our lives because of our testimony. What we did not anticipate is that this might be repeated in our relationships with church members. Some Christians have discovered that changing attendance from church A to church B is to be rejected by their former friends in church A.

This rejection is especially severe when there has been a separation in the congregation. Those who left to begin an assembly of their own are often treated as worse than heathen, while the founders of the new church justify their actions by rejecting the old congregation as being rigidly religious. In either case, the pain of rejection goes deep into the souls of those involved.

When the Prodigal Son returned home, the enthusiastic reception by his father was totally unexpected. However, his restoration to the full privileges of sonship and the joyful welcome-home banquet were marred for him by the rejection of his elder brother. He was not prepared for the deep, unresolved anger his brother had nursed over the years he had been gone.

We Christians are equally shocked when our brothers and sisters in Christ reject us because we fail to meet some standard of righteousness or perfection they have set for us. If we don't see eschatology the way they see it, they repudiate us. Should our concept of holiness fail to match theirs, they spurn us. This rejection hurts deeply.

Christians seem to find it difficult to allow for differences and variety in one another. We feel threatened by anyone who is unlike us, so we reject them. Instead of contributing to the peace and life of the Church, we contribute to the hurt and pain of fellow believers. We function in the law of similarity instead of the law of love. Jesus did not say that being exactly the same would be the mark of discipleship. What He did say was:

> By this shall all men know that ye are my disciples,
> if ye have love one to another. (John 13:35)

Love does not hurt — it heals. It is rare for us to see marriage partners who are alike. Somehow opposites tend to attract, for love often flows best through opposites. How sad that this rarely seems true in our Christian relationships. In every fresh visitation of God to His Church, there are members who move in the fresh revelation, and others who prefer to remain in the former visitation God gave to their parents. Love seldom continues to flow between the two factions. Instead of drawing strength from one another, they denounce each other as either heretical or historical, and each inflicts pain upon the other.

Further development in Christ demands that these wounds be healed. We need to come to Jesus with the prayer, "Lord, it's me, hurting from rejection. Please receive me, and make me know that I am welcome in Your presence." This will begin a healing process that can restore wholeness to us in our daily living.

It's Me, Hurting from Failure

When I responded as a boy to the call of God to enter the ministry, I felt absolutely certain that I would never fail. After all, wasn't it the Lord Himself who was inviting me to join Him in this service? Now with sixty-plus years of service behind me, I realize that it was youthful idealism that caused me to believe I could be flawless. The truth is, I have failed repeatedly. I have led congregations toward a vision that I was convinced was of God, only to have to admit painful failure and call for an "about face!"

All failure in Christian service is pain-producing. It is doubly so if that failure hurt anyone who was involved with us. Not all building programs run smoothly, and not all mission projects prove successful. Sometimes unforeseen problems stop a project before its completion, and collected funds cannot be recovered and returned.

The disciples knew the pain of failure in their Christian service. They had earlier exercised great power and authority over demons when Jesus sent them out two-by-two. While

Jesus was on the Mount of Transfiguration with Peter, James, and John, a father brought his demonized son to the disciples. They found themselves completely powerless to cast out these demons. It was an embarrassing, frustrating and hurtful experience for them.

We, too, have known this kind of failure in our ministries. We have prayed for the sick according to the Word of God, only to have to bury them a short while later. Many Christians have given up all attempts at exercising authority over the demons because of repeated failures they have experienced.

It is difficult to rise above the pain of failure when ministering to the public. Our self-confidence weakens, our faith fails, and our pride is deeply wounded. It is easy to expect failure instead of success. We often set ourselves up for failure. We react to our pain and we seek to prevent further hurt.

A friend of mine became the pastor of a distressed church in one of our major cities at the insistence of the elders of the congregation. As the church began to heal and grow, he felt a need for more help and sought a young man to serve as an assistant pastor. After carefully checking the references of several candidates, he settled on one candidate and was thrilled to see him bring many young people into the church. After a while, however, this young man and his youthful followers staged an uprising to replace the senior pastor and take over the leadership of the church. It was a long, painful confrontation that ended in a split congregation.

The wounds in this encounter went so deep that the pastor could not bring himself to minister to the remaining members of the congregation for many weeks. He felt he had failed them by bringing this young man on staff to serve with him. He constantly chastened himself by saying, "I made the greatest mistake of my life."

About three months after the insurrection, a remaining

67

staff member approached the pastor with a cassette tape in his hand. "Do you remember the prophecy that the visiting evangelist spoke over you many months ago?"

"Well, I do remember hearing the prophecy, but I don't remember what it said," the pastor responded.

Handing the tape to the pastor the man said, "I just ran across it while working in the tape department. I think you should listen to it."

The pastor told me that this word God had given to him at least two months before the trouble erupted clearly told him that trouble was coming, but that he, the pastor, had made no mistake. God said that He was allowing this coming trouble to do a separating and purging work in the congregation.

Perhaps if this pastor had really heard the prophecy when it was given, it would have prevented much of the deep hurt he experienced. He told me that when he listened to the recording, peace replaced the pain and he could pick up his ministerial responsibilities again.

We also experience deep pain in failed personal relationships. Despite what was stated as the reason for divorce, there is a tremendous sense of failure in the lives of the divorced persons when the decree becomes final. Similarly, when a friendship deteriorates, it produces wounds that hurt.

All failures produce hurt in us, whether these failures are in the areas of service, relationships or personal righteousness. We set out on this Christian adventure intending to succeed. We don't know what to do with failure, but Jesus does. He handled Peter's failure with the simple message, "Go, tell . . . Peter that I'll meet him in Galilee." All Peter needed to know was that failure on his part did not sever his relationship with God. We dare not let our failures drive us from God. We need to let them drive us back to God to find out how to rise above them and to succeed the second time.

What can we do when we hurt so deeply? Perhaps the

worst thing we can do is to seek out another hurting person to compare wounds. We may get a few comforting words in that encounter, but we won't get healed. We are like the situation in Jeremiah's day:

> They have healed also the hurt of the daughter of my people slightly, saying, Peace, peace; when there is no peace. (Jeremiah 6:14)

False hope is not what we need. Platitudes and pity may give temporary emotional release, but they are not healing aids. We need greater help than these can bring. There are five things that can heal our inner hurts:

1. A fresh awareness of Jesus
2. A realization that we need healing
3. A commitment to prayer
4. A dedication to Bible reading
5. A rapport with a pastor

First, we need to remind ourselves that Jesus lives in eternity. He transcends all time. He was there when we were wounded, but He did not rush in to prevent it, for that would have violated the human will. He does not desire to make puppets of any of us. But His full knowledge of the circumstances makes it easier for Him to heal our wounds. It also helps to remember that:

> He was wounded for our transgressions, he was bruised for our iniquities: the chastisement of our peace was upon him; and with his stripes we are healed. (Isaiah 53:6)

The abuse He bore was to enable Him to help us in our hurts and sorrows, and whatever caused them.

Second, we will not be healed of our inner wounds until

we admit to ourselves, and sometimes to others, that we need to be healed. It isn't until we face the reality of our need that we are willing to invest the time and energy it will require to bring healing to our inner nature.

Third, we must make a commitment to pray. We must cry, "Lord, it's me, hurting again. Please heal me." It helps if we will:

> Tell God every detail of your needs in earnest and thankful prayer, and the peace of God, which transcends human understanding, will keep constant guard over your hearts and minds as they rest in Christ Jesus. (Philippians 4:6, J. B. Phillips' translation.)

We must talk our hurts over with God; He is a good listener. When we let Him talk to us, we discover that He is also a divine counselor. If we could help ourselves, we wouldn't be hurting. Isn't it time we disciplined ourselves to pray and allow Jesus to help us?

A fourth step to healing our inner hurts is to spend time reading the Bible daily. The Bible is God's communication to us, and we need to hear from God. This book is a great source of comfort, and it functions as the manufacturer's instruction book for our lives. There is no more valuable book in the world, but it cannot help us unless we read it.

A fifth step to healing is to have an acceptable rapport with a pastor. They are God's gifts to Christians. A concerned pastor can often direct us away from hurtful situations into a more healthy walk in life. His sympathetic listening, his compassionate sensing of our wounded spirit and his comforting prayers go a long way in bringing us to spiritual and emotional wholeness. Our tears can be dried sufficiently enough for us to come to the Father with our petitions.

6

Lord, It's Me, Petitioning Again

A Change of Requesting

No one doubts that the Prodigal Son had lots of things to ask his father, but the most important question on his mind was a petition to be received back onto the farm, even if he could be accepted at a level no higher than a servant. He did not know if he had a basis for his petition, but his need was so great that he dared to reach for the old relationship he had experienced with his father for so many years as he was growing up on the farm. He combined his need with his knowledge of his father's nature. That is the true basis for petitioning our heavenly Father.

We are not unaware of our needs, although we often mistake a desire as being a true need. We need not be ignorant of our Father's nature, for He has consistently revealed Himself as loving, forgiving and generous. Jesus told us:

> Whatsoever ye shall ask in prayer, believing, ye shall receive . . . Ask, and ye shall receive, that your joy may be full. (Matthew 21:22; John 16:4)

71

I have repeatedly told pastors, "If you face a difficulty in your congregation, ask a recent convert to pray about it. God consistently grants their requests." Perhaps this is because they have a fresh flow of faith. We teach them that God answers prayer, so they pray. Just as children believe their parents, new Christians believe their God. They do not have any failures nagging at their conscious minds, so their confidence remains unshaken. The very simplicity with which they pray is inspiring to hear. It is such a contrast to the religious people who often preach a prayer instead of simply talking to God.

There may also be a divine side to such instant response to the prayers of new converts. Like an infant, their survival is totally dependent upon the care of another during the initial season of their Christian experience. Since so few churches accept parental responsibilities for new converts, God mercifully responds to their every petition just as a tender parent responds to every cry of his or her new son or daughter. There is an awareness that the parent is the total life-support system for the baby. Since the New Testament declares that we are "born of God" (1 John 4:7), it is natural that God accepts a paternal responsibility over us.

After more than half a century of preaching, I can attest that new converts pray almost as instinctively as a baby cries. They may not have a strong theological concept of God, but experientially, they seem to know that:

> And it shall come to pass, that before they call, I will answer; and while they are yet speaking, I will hear. (Isaiah 65:24)

They do not pray for the psychological release that telling problems to another can bring. They pray because they need help beyond themselves, and they genuinely believe that God will help them. And He does! He always has a warm bottle ready.

To balance this infant stage where it seems that the

Christian convert is in charge of God, there is a fundamental principle in God's world called progressive maturity. Nothing remains a baby forever. If it does, it is horribly deformed. Everything God created matures from a seed to a seed producer. Just as the acorn produces the oak tree that grows acorns, the infant will become mature enough to eventually give birth to another infant. This is evident in both the human and the spiritual realms. The Old and the New Testaments teach that there will be progressive growth and maturity in God's children.

> But unto you that fear my name shall the Sun of righteousness arise with healing in his wings; and ye shall go forth, and grow up as calves of the stall. (Malachi 4:2)

> But speaking the truth in love, may grow up into him in all things, which is the head, even Christ. (Ephesians 4:15)

Self-dependence comes with spiritual maturity. New converts become more and more self-sufficient. They discover that God will not do for them what He has enabled them to do for themselves, and they find great satisfaction in being able to put on their shoes and feed themselves. There are bragging rights in achieving such spiritual maturity.

Unfortunately, however, early maturity often brings on independence. Because they can now do what they once asked God to do for them, there comes a feeling that they don't presently need God's help. They rejoice fully in His past work, but they misunderstand self-dependence in fundamentals for independence in all things. They accept maturity to a teenage level in their walk with God as full maturity in Christian experience.

None of us is in greater danger than when we declare ourselves independent from God. Paul told the audience on Mars Hill in Athens, Greece:

> For in him we live, and move, and have our being;
> as certain also of your own poets have said, For we are
> also his offspring. (Acts 17:28)

We may not depend perpetually upon God for a bottle, but we permanently depend on Him for the life we live. When we sever ourselves from the life of God, we die.

Maturity should not bring independence from God. It simply makes us aware of our dependence on Him at higher levels. Whereas we once called upon Him exclusively for physical needs, as we matured, we discovered that our spiritual needs were greater than our physical ones and that we were incapable of meeting those needs alone. We don't need God any less; we need Him in different areas of our lives. We begin to see a greater depth in Paul's promise:

> But my God shall supply all your need according to
> his riches in glory by Christ Jesus. (Philippians 4:19)

Whereas we used to approach this verse with our checkbooks and deposit slips in hand, we begin to realize that we have needs that can never be met by finances alone. This is often frustrating to the developing Christian.

For a lengthy season, new believers need do little more than whine or cry to have their needs met by God. As they learn to meet these needs for themselves, they discover needs at higher levels in their lives, and realize that crying won't bring them an answer. Like the maturing child in the home, they have to learn to relate to the Father differently than they had related to Him before.

It's Me Again, Learning to Pray

How selfish our initial prayers were. They were almost exclusively "I" centered. The consistent theme was "I, me, we" as we prayed for health, wealth, and happiness. Childlike as we were, the Christian world revolved around us.

No one condemns a small child for being selfish, nor does God censure a new convert for asking in a self-centered fashion. Yet as the children grow older, quality parents seek to move them from extreme self-centeredness to an extended awareness of others. God does this with His children.

It is interesting that when the disciples asked Jesus to teach them to pray, He instructed them to pray for God's glory before He showed them how to petition God for personal needs. He told them:

> After this manner therefore pray ye: Our Father which art in heaven, Hallowed be thy name. Thy kingdom come. Thy will be done in earth, as it is in heaven. (Matthew 6:9-10)

Was Jesus suggesting that God would not be hallowed without their praying, or that God's kingdom could not be established without their petitions? Hardly! There is nothing a person can do that will change the name and nature of God, nor does God need our permission to establish His reign on earth. Recognizing the developing spiritual maturity of these men, Jesus sought to elevate their level of prayer. He wanted them to lift their eyes to God and off of themselves. It was an initial step out of self-centered praying. It helped them to put God in the center of their spiritual universe. It was a big step into mature praying.

It is threatening when God begins to nudge us out of lower levels of prayer. We are always uncomfortable with anything new, and when the new way changes our focus, great insecurities are created. If we revert to our old ways, we discover that they no longer work and it devastates us. We interpret it as rejection.

It is natural to feel rejected when previous methods of

prayer cease to be productive. Sensitive people will go inward looking for sin and failure. Their hearts condemn them, even though they can find no obvious sin from which to repent. Others, who are less sensitive, may blame God, declaring that God has abandoned them. Neither the attitude of rejection or abandonment is correct.

God's Word assures us that our prayers are heard, even when our sensitive hearts try to condemn us. John wrote:

> For if our heart condemn us, God is greater than our heart, and knoweth all things. Beloved, if our heart condemn us not, then have we confidence toward God. And whatsoever we ask, we receive of him, because we keep his commandments, and do those things that are pleasing in his sight. (1 John 3:20-22)

Whether or not our hearts condemn us, God remains unchanged. He listens to all our prayers in spite of our failures, but sometimes He delays His answer until we have prayed more properly. It is for our development that God urges us to higher levels of communion with Him.

When my daughters were children, I was content to have them talk to me in very simple sentences about very common things. As they entered high school, I expected compound sentences about far more complex topics. Now that they are married and have become mothers, the subject matter about which they talk and the way they talk about it, is far more mature than when they were in school. Our fellowship is now at its highest level.

If God allowed it, some of us would talk baby talk all the way into eternity. But He will not allow this. He uses the silent treatment to make us restate our prayers. He fails to immediately respond to immature praying if He knows the praying person is capable of a higher level of communication.

When we discover that our former crying, whining and complaining does not get the same results it previously did, we need to relearn prayer. Like the child who is being taught to say "please," and "thank you," we have to learn a new approach to God. We begin to respect His will and His ways when approaching Him with our wants and our wishes. We mature sufficiently to see Father God as a person rather than a providing power. We discover that prayer is communication between two persons, not merely a wish list sent to a spiritual "Santa Claus." Paul implied this when he told the Corinthian believers:

> When I was a child, I spake as a child, I understood as a child, I thought as a child: but when I became a man, I put away childish things. (1 Corinthians 13:11)

Prayer, which is communication with God, must mature in nature as our natures mature. Childish prayers belong to children, but are distasteful in spiritually mature adults. Our approach to God should match our affiliation with Him. Our approach was initially out of need, but now our access is through relationship. In our childish ignorance, God responded to us at any level of faith we exercised. But as we come to know Him more fully, He insists that we make our approach through Jesus with a full complement of faith.

Because we will continue to mature until Jesus returns, we need to consistently enlarge our capacity to pray. Perhaps we need to join David in praying:

> Lead me in thy truth, and teach me: for thou art the God of my salvation; on thee do I wait all the day. (Psalms 25:5)

Higher levels of prayer are no longer instinctive reactions. We have to be led into them and have them taught to us by the Lord. Paying careful attention to His instruction will bring us to greater seasons of prayer. As we live our Christian lives, we will repeatedly find ourselves praying,

"Lord, here I am again, learning to pray." He always proves to be a great teacher.

It's Me Again, Learning to Ask

Once he determined to return home, the biggest problem the Prodigal Son faced was in determining how to talk to his father. Until he had left home, his father had met his every need. He had even granted the request to divide the family inheritance before the father's death. Now, however, the son knew that his relationship with the father was different. The life he had lived while separated from home had changed this son.

As the Prodigal Son torturously retraced his steps homeward, he rehearsed in his mind what he would say when he saw his father. He finally settled on the simple request:

> I will arise and go to my father, and will say unto him, Father, I have sinned against heaven, and before thee, And am no more worthy to be called thy son: make me as one of thy hired servants. (Luke 15:18-19)

This was a confession of sin, of broken relationship and of complete unworthiness. He admitted to himself that he had wasted all previous gifts of the father. He sought restoration at any level of acceptance the father could give to him.

As a young man, the son had wanted possessions; the more mature man wanted position. What had been so important in his youth seemed less important in his manhood. The earlier petitions had been for riches. The later plea was for a relationship. In his less mature days, his petition had been "give me." Now, both older and wiser, he determined to pray, "make me." While we do not condone his behavior, we can understand that it matured him.

We need not play the role of the Prodigal Son to see

similar changes in our requests to our heavenly Father as we mature. There was a day when we yearned for the product of God's farm. When we had spent it all, we began to yearn for the father and the farm that produced what we once wanted. Our early petitions had been very selfish. We yearned for things, pleasure and spiritual toys, but as we matured in God, our relationship with Him became more important than any gifts He could give to us.

Many Christians have painfully learned that no matter how lavishly the Father bestows His gifts upon them, they will be wasted when used away from His presence. It is the elder son, who stays in relationship with the father on the farm, who can multiply the wealth of his father, and because he is heir to the estate, his own wealth.

Had the Prodigal Son used the same approach he had used when he was younger, it is likely that he would have received nothing. But because his approach was more mature, he received far more from his father than he dared to ask, and so do we. Our needs are met by God when we ask out of pure motives in a mature manner.

We need to learn to pray at every level of maturity, and we need to know how to ask and what to ask for as we age in Christ. No wonder we so often come to the Lord saying, "It's me again, learning to ask."

Prayer is an action that brings the promised answer. Sometimes we fall into the trap of believing that just because God promised it, we automatically have it. It is important to learn again to ask, for we are no longer infants whose needs are automatically met. It is equally important to learn how to ask, for James told us:

> Ye have not, because ye ask not. Ye ask, and receive not, because ye ask amiss, that ye may consume it upon your lusts. (James 4:2-3)

We go without because we do not request, or we are denied because of impure motivations. We simply need to relearn to pray. God pledged through His prophet:

> Call unto me, and I will answer thee, and shew thee great and mighty things, which thou knowest not. (Jeremiah 33:3)

Obviously, prayer is not limited by location, for Jeremiah was in prison when he wrote this. The prophet Jonah prayed fervently from the belly of a great fish. Furthermore, prayer is not hindered by negative circumstances. We may pray from lives of ease and comfort or from lives filled with tension, anxiety or pain. In either case, God has bound Himself to hear and to respond to our prayers.

It seems obvious that the purpose of prayer is to gain an audience with God. To know that God exists is great; to be a friend of God is splendid, but to be able to have an audience with Almighty God is supreme! The initiative for that audience is ours — "You call and I will answer thee" is His pledge to us.

It's Me Again, Learning to Repeat

If prayer is asking, answered prayer must be receiving. If we do not hear from God, we have cut the prayer time too short. We've made a monologue out of what should have been a dialogue. God declares that He wants to answer us, so we should not cease asking until we hear from Him.

Some Christians fear that asking a second or third time is evidence of a lack of faith, but the Lord taught us that it shows an importunity of faith. Jesus praised the widow who came to the judge repeatedly until she got justice, and then He applied it to us by saying:

> And shall not God avenge his own elect, which cry
> day and night unto him, though he bear long with them?
> I tell you that he will avenge them speedily. Nevertheless
> when the Son of man cometh, shall he find faith on the
> earth? (Luke 18:6-8)

There are other Christians who feel that repeating the same prayer to God will be viewed as an attempt to overrule the divine will. If God says "no!" to a petition that, of course, should settle it. Nagging God won't change His mind. Much of the time, however, we petition and receive no communication from God. That is our clue to repeat the request. The reason for repeating our petitions is not simply to get God's attention. Jesus told us:

> But when ye pray, use not vain repetitions, as the
> heathen do: for they think that they shall be heard for
> their much speaking. Be not ye therefore like unto them:
> for your Father knoweth what things ye have need of,
> before ye ask him. (Matthew 6:7-8)

God is neither hard of hearing nor inattentive. He has not programmed heaven's computer to answer the person who calls in the most frequently. "Vain repetitions," as Jesus calls them, gain us no points with God. Nor do we need to repeat our requests for fear God did not understand our expressed need. Jesus assures us that even before we ask Him, God knows what we need.

What, then, is the value of learning to repeat our petitions? Asking repeatedly does far more for us than it does for God. He knows that giving to us before we are truly ready to receive contributes to our weaknesses instead of our well-being. In our repeated requesting, we effect changes in ourselves, our attitudes, actions and aspirations. In seeking to find a reason for unanswered prayer, we make adjustments in our motives and manners. This praying greatly influences our lives.

Through the years, we have heard preaching on both sides

of the question: "Does prayer influence God?" Each side has its strengths. Prayer does not influence God's *purpose*, but it does influence God's *performance*. God's plans were settled long before the foundations of the world were laid, and our present praying will not influence those purposes. God's actions, however, are greatly influenced by our asking. When we learn His purposes and make them our prayers, we give God the opportunity to act in our lives.

In another sense, prayer enables God to do for us without damaging us in any way. Suppose, for the moment, that God is thinking about us and planning, with His predetermined love plans, to give us much that He possesses. Yet in His wisdom, He refrains from giving because we do not know our own needs and have not opened our hands and hearts to receive from Him. Even if He poured it out, we could not receive it.

Perhaps God realizes that in not knowing our true needs, we might abuse, misuse or fail to use His gift. He waits in tenderness until we become personally aware of that and we begin to talk to Him about it. When our awareness of a need becomes sufficient enough that we ask God to meet that need, God, in His delight with the change in us, joyfully gives us the petition we have requested. We have finally asked Him to do what He has been desiring to do. We are finally praying in the perfect will of God.

Our first glimpse of what we lacked caused us to pray, but it was our continued praying that expanded our awareness of our need. Had we asked only one time, we would never have obtained it, but in our continual asking, He was able to prepare our hearts and lives to receive and release His gift.

Much of the praying in this generation is anemic and diminutive because our concept of God and His ways is so puny. We need great understanding to be able to pray great prayers. To "ask great and mighty things" (see Jeremiah 33:3), we need great and mighty visions. These cannot be self-induced. They must come from God Himself.

The promise that God gave through Jeremiah ("Call unto me, and I will answer thee") not only assures us that Jehovah will hear and respond, but it also pledges this needed enlargement to us. "I will show thee great and mighty things" is God's statement. Over twenty verses of the Bible say, "I will show thee . . . ." The prophet Daniel was in prayer every time a divine revelation came to him. The Apostle Paul speaks of being in prayer when revelation came to him. This was true of Abraham, David, and many others. God revealed great things to them when they were in communication with Him. John reported that when he was on the Isle of Patmos:

> I looked, and, behold, a door was opened in heaven: and the first voice which I heard was as it were of a trumpet talking with me; which said, Come up hither, and I will shew thee things which must be hereafter. (Revelation 4:1)

The revelation God purposed to give to John demanded a connection between earth and heaven, and prayer was that connection. Since prayer is a two-way communication between God and man, it becomes the chief channel for revelation.

God reveals His will, His Word, and His work through our prayer channel. He also reveals our self, our sin, and our stubbornness when we are in prayer communication with Him. He reveals His provision in the past, His plan for the present, and His purpose for the future through the prayer channel. If we need a revelation of or from God, we must get into a place of prayer and stay there until He shows "the thing which thou knowest not."

Wisely do we cry, "Lord, it's me again, learning to pray, to ask and to repeat." As a by-product of this, we begin to restore ourselves in body, soul and spirit. Like the Prodigal Son, we initially hoped to become a servant, but our restoration brought us to restored sonship.

7

Lord, It's Me, Restoring Again

A Change of Position

Long before he hit the pigpen, the Prodigal Son yearned to be restored. Somewhat like David when he fled before his enemies, this son could also lament:

> Therefore is my spirit overwhelmed within me; my heart within me is desolate. I remember the days of old; I meditate on all thy works; I muse on the work of thy hands. I stretch forth my hands unto thee: my soul thirsteth after thee, as a thirsty land. Selah. (Psalms 13:4-6)

The deep desire of his heart was to somehow be restored, and he eventually reasoned that he would have to be active in this restoration. He could not expect the father to go looking for him and offer restoration.

It is a divine work of God's grace that restores our inner natures. Our Christian experiences would wear out and perish early in our walk with God without it. As David said:

> The LORD is my shepherd; I shall not want. He maketh me to lie down in green pastures: he leadeth me beside the still waters. He restoreth my soul: he leadeth

me in the paths of righteousness for his name's sake. (Psalms 23:1-3)

"He restoreth my soul" goes beyond mere hope of continued life and ministry. We need to be restored daily, for just as daily living exhausts our physical bodies, so our spiritual natures need to be replenished. Paul realized this, for he wrote:

> For which cause we faint not; but though our outward man perish, yet the inward man is renewed day by day. (2 Corinthians 4:16)

God is the restorer of our souls, and I have lived long enough to recognize the place that personal involvement plays in this restoration. It is not God's fault that some people shine as constantly as the North Star while others simply blaze a brief, but fiery path across the dark winter sky. He plans and builds for eternity. Even fragile plant life has a built-in continuity through its roots and seeds. Nothing about God is short-term. His goal is to restore and to replenish.

If restoration is totally a work of God, why are so many earnest Christians devitalized in faith and hope, depleted in spiritual power and dissipated in physical and emotional energy? Is God capricious in preserving some and exhausting others? Anyone who has met God knows that He is not fickle; He is meticulous and meritorious. His work is not based on privilege, but on promise. What He has made available to one person is available to all.

What many people lack is a personal participation in God's plan of restoration. David's Shepherd Psalm beautifully declares that God "restoreth my soul." None would dispute that statement, but anyone familiar with sheep knows that the shepherd cannot do this by himself. The process of this restoration is to bring the sheep to a protected place of abundant provision. There they can rest from the strain of moving from one pasture to another. The shepherd has provided food and water, but the sheep must eat and drink.

Some Christians want to be restored by a sovereign act of God. They want Him to feed them intravenously. They seek restoration by having a man of God lay hands on them to impart spiritual renewal. That is not the way the Great Shepherd restores our soul. He provides us with the protection of His presence, the food of His Word, the water of His Spirit and the fellowship of His flock and says, "Be restored." Only those sheep who participate and partake of these provisions will be renewed. The others can perish in the midst of plenty.

In the days of sailing vessels, a severe storm on the Atlantic Ocean blew a passenger ship, coming to America from England, far off its course. The intensity of the storm washed most of the fresh water supply overboard. In the calm days that followed the storm, the ship sat almost motionless in the sea; its sails lying limp against the mast, while the passengers languished for water. A few of the weaker persons died of thirst and had to be buried at sea.

In desperation, one of the sailors lowered a bucket into the sea, intending to drink sea water, though he knew its salt content would actually hasten his dehydration. To his amazement, the water was completely fresh! No one knew that the ship had been sitting for days in the fresh water of the mighty Amazon River of South America that extends into the ocean far beyond sight of land. People were dying of thirst while floating in the confluence of the mightiest river in the world!

Too many Christians perish for lack of the Living Water of the Holy Spirit while actually surrounded and buoyed by His presence. We cry out, "God, where are You when I need You?" completely ignoring His affirmation, "I will never leave thee, nor forsake thee" (Hebrews 13:5). The problem is

87

not His presence, but our awareness and appropriation of that presence.

"He restoreth my soul" is a provision and not merely a principle. It is an availability, but it is not automatic. Even in this we are "workers together with him" (2 Corinthians. 6:1). This is why I visualize myself coming into God's presence to say, "Lord, it's me, restoring again!" I find this healthier than the desperate prayer, "Lord, restore me anew," for this usually makes me a passive non-participant.

My very entrance into God's presence begins a process of restoration. In my awareness of need, I come to the source of supply. My obvious weakness makes it imperative that I return to my source of spiritual strength. It is in His pasture, not in the world's pleasure, that I am renewed.

God gave a promise of restoration to Israel through the prophet Joel, and through its quotation in the Book of Acts, to the Church. God said:

> And I will restore to you the years that the locust hath eaten, the cankerworm, and the caterpillar, and the palmerworm, my great army which I sent among you. (Joel 2:25)

Whatever our locust may be (the cankerworm, caterpillar and palmerworm are simply developing stages of the locust), God promises to provide restoration from their devastation. Whether it is living, ministering or fighting the enemy that has depleted us, God has provided restoration for our souls. After a serious bout with sin, David cried to God:

> Restore unto me the joy of thy salvation; and uphold me with thy free spirit. (Psalms 51:12)

This worshiping king knew that as he returned to the secret place of God's presence, he could have his joy restored to his life.

Modern Christians need to embrace this same confidence. Whatever the reason for the loss of joy, strength, trust or anointing, "He restoreth." We are foolish to order spiritual wheelchairs when God offers renewed strength with which to "walk in the Spirit." David testified:

> Who satisfieth thy mouth with good things; so that thy youth is renewed like the eagle's. (Psalms 103:5)

This is why I dare to say, "Lord, it's me, restoring again." I am joining in God's great program of restoration, and I choose to be an active participant.

It's Me, Recharging Again

I disliked having to leave right after speaking in the afternoon session during a conference in the South, but I had a plane to catch. I was the keynote speaker at a worship conference in the Chicago area yet that evening, and with a stopover, it was a three-hour flight. I knew my schedule was tight, for after arriving at Chicago's very busy airport, I was still almost an hour's drive from the church, but if all went well, I could go directly from the plane to the church.

It was encouraging to have the plane arrive at O'Hare Field five minutes early and as I deplaned, it pleased me to see the sponsoring pastor waiting for me as I exited the jetway. He was a good walker and the two of us quickly covered the long distance to the baggage return area. My luggage arrived within minutes and I fastened the cases onto my portable luggage cart and followed the pastor through the labyrinth of corridors to the parking garage.

As we placed the luggage in the church van, I rejoiced inwardly for the remarkable speed we had achieved in getting to the van. We were at least ten minutes ahead of my mental schedule.

We fastened our seat belts and the pastor inserted the key into the ignition and turned it to engage the starter. Instead of hearing the engine turn over, we heard a disheartening "click-click." He repeatedly tried to start the van, but his efforts produced nothing but a "click-click." Even opening the hood and jiggling the wires didn't change anything. We had a dead battery and were stranded.

The pastor was, understandably, embarrassed. He explained to me that he had experienced no battery problem with the van before this. He also pointed out that he carried jumper cables, but we soon discovered that the people coming to our level of this vast parking garage were in too great a hurry to help us.

Leaving me in the van on a night that broke the existing low temperature record for that time of the year, the pastor went searching for help. He returned much later and explained that O'Hare Airport provides emergency service, and that he had phoned for help. "They should be here momentarily," he said. Unfortunately for us, "momentarily" proved to be thirty minutes.

The driver of the emergency truck finally arrived and parked next to our van, pulled out the jumper cables and tried to help us, but the engine compartment was so crowded, the mechanic couldn't make a good connection. He tried repeatedly, but he was unsuccessful. Finally the pastor succeeded in connecting the cables and the engine was successfully jump-started back to life.

With a grateful "thank you" to the service man, we headed out of the garage, but by now the church service had begun. All my rush, push and anxiety of that day was wasted. It was now obvious that we would miss the evening service because we had lacked the power to get the engine going. Instead of speaking in the convention, I arrived at my motel about 10:00 p.m.

They had scheduled me for this conference two years

earlier. They had even sent me the money for the ticket six months in advance, but a shortage of electrical energy prevented the fulfillment of my commission.

Jesus both authorized and energized His disciples. He never sends us to minister with a dead battery. We read in the Gospel account:

> Then He called his twelve disciples together and gave them power and authority over all demons, and to cure diseases. (Luke 9:1)

The Greek word we have translated "power" is *dunamis*. It means strength or mighty works. The word for "authority" is *exousia*, meaning right or authority. In His name, we have both legal authority and spiritual energy over the kingdom of Satan.

Any commission from God contains a capability for fulfilling it. God never exhorts us to action without energizing us for that action. Jesus told the disciples before His ascension:

> But ye shall receive power, [*dunamis*] after that the Holy Ghost is come upon you: and ye shall be witnesses unto me both in Jerusalem, and in all Judaea, and in Samaria, and unto the uttermost part of the earth. (Acts 1:8)

Divine ability consistently accompanies commissioned action. God does not expect us to function in divine ministries through human energies. His *dunamis* [the root for our word dynamite] accompanies His delegation.

Why, then, do we often find ourselves powerless to perform the action Christ has commanded? Perhaps we have failed to recharge the battery. Joseph Parker, the English divine of a past generation, said: "Men no longer have the thunder because they have lost the lightning." We can't have one without the other.

Jesus was on His way to heal the daughter of Jairus when a woman with a continuous flow of blood secretly touched the hem of His garment and was completely healed.

> And Jesus said, Who touched me? When all denied, Peter and they that were with him said, Master, the multitude throng thee and press thee, and sayest thou, Who touched me? And Jesus said, Somebody hath touched me: for I perceive that virtue [*dunamis*] is gone out of me. (Luke 8:44-45)

Jesus was aware when divine power flowed from Him to another person. Anytime another person receives spiritual energy from us, we lose it. We tend to forget that the repeated command of Jesus was:

> Give, and it shall be given unto you; good measure, pressed down, and shaken together, and running over, shall men give into your bosom. For with the same measure that ye mete withal it shall be measured to you again. (Luke 6:38)

It is impossible to give and yet retain possession. This is why we must learn to return to our source to be recharged after all seasons of ministry. Otherwise we will find ourselves with a depleted battery. When Paul wrote to the very active church in Ephesus, he challenged these Christians:

> And be not drunk with wine, wherein is excess; but be filled with the Spirit. (Ephesians 5:18)

The tense of the Greek needs a translation, "Keep being filled with the Spirit." It refers to a progressive work, not to the initial infilling of the Spirit. All the spiritual activity for which Christ commended this church in His letter to them in Chapter 2 of Revelation demanded that they have a continuing flow of the Holy Spirit. We may not live in Ephesus, but we need this same emphasis. We, too, need to cry: "Lord, it's me again, plugging in to get recharged for service."

It's Me, Recycling Again

America has become a throw-away society. We have viewed our resources as limitless for too long, and we replace rather than repair. Also, manufacturers have a planned obsolescence for their products, and their advertising creates in us a desire for the new even if the old is still working.

Now we are being told that we are rapidly running out of space to bury our displaced articles. Our government is seriously attempting to reeducate us. Never have Americans been made more aware of the need to recycle than at the present. All forms of the media urge us to return our used aluminum cans, salvage our newspapers, and reuse our plastic bags. Even our schools are teaching the students that our resources are no longer limitless and must be reused.

Christians must apply this same principle to their spiritual lives. God's economy has never been a throw-away economy. He is the original recycler. All nature proves this. The seed of the plant reproduces that plant. The fallen tree decays and enriches the soil, making the growth of a replacement tree that much easier. Even the human body will heal itself if given a chance.

If, as Paul teaches, God's method of instruction is "first the natural then the spiritual" (see 1 Corinthians 15:46), God's plan of reclamation for nature should apply to the spiritual. We need to learn that broken lives can be magnificently mended by the Spirit of God. There is no life so damaged by sin that God's Spirit is unable to reclaim it. Isn't this the fundamental message of the story of the Prodigal Son?

Perhaps if the Church used the term "recycled" instead of "redeemed," we might better understand God's glorious work of salvation. This is what God taught Jeremiah when He sent him to the potter's house where he saw the craftsman trying to form a vessel out of the spinning clay. (See Jeremiah 18.) When the artist found an unyielding lump in the clay, he did not discard it. He returned it to the kneading trough and softened it. Then he replaced the clay on the wheel and formed it into another vessel. The potter recycled that clay. Aren't we recycled?

We also have to remind ourselves that empty vessels can be refilled instead of being replaced. We turn out graduates from our Bible schools and seminaries as replacements for exhausted, burned-out pastors instead of realizing that God can renew those vessels and fill them again with His Holy Spirit. While it is true that youth will be served, it is equally true that age has broad experience to offer.

God did not discard Paul when, after years of service, he began to spend more time in crude prisons than in church pulpits. While in prison, Paul could not preach with the great power that had made him so useful to God's kingdom, but this didn't seem to distress God. He merely refilled Paul and gave him the capacity to write spiritual truth. Most of our New Testament came to us through this recycled apostle.

I hear some people lament that they didn't give themselves to Christ's service as a young person. I rejoice to see others enter retirement with a cry in their spirit, "What can I do for God?" Many of these have gone to the mission field as builders, teachers, helpers and associates to resident missionaries. Others have gone to Bible school and have entered the evangelistic field here at home. They were convinced that God could recycle them even in their aging years. They saw themselves as strong bottles that could be filled with another product and made available to people.

God does not require new people to make available a new

easier when someone else directs it and accepts responsibility for it.

The Psalmist understood the provision God made for resting. It is written:

> Rest in the LORD, and wait patiently for him: fret not thyself because of him who prospereth in his way, because of the man who bringeth wicked devices to pass . . . Return unto thy rest, O my soul; for the LORD hath dealt bountifully with thee. (Psalms 37:7; 116:7)

One evidence of Christian maturity is entering into God's rest. When we learn to trust the grace of God and lean upon the strength of God, we cease trying to save ourselves and find a rest in the completed work of God for our lives. The author of the Book of Hebrews says:

> There remaineth therefore a rest to the people of God. For he that is entered into his rest, he also hath ceased from his own works, as God did from his. Let us labour therefore to enter into that rest, lest any man fall after the same example of unbelief. (Hebrews 4:9-11)

How easy it is for us to get on a treadmill of religious activity and never get off. Perhaps it is rooted in our unwillingness to accept our humanity. Our desire for Christian perfection causes us to discount our true nature, and we try to function as miniature gods. Even the indwelling Holy Spirit does not transform a mortal into an immortal. We are redeemed persons, not reclaimed angels. The work of Christ at the cross deals with the sin that separated us from God, but it does not dispense with our humanity.

Our bodies become exhausted. Our souls get weary, and even our spirits experience fatigue during the pressures of daily living. Under great pressure, David admitted:

> Therefore is my spirit overwhelmed within me; my heart within me is desolate . . . Hear me speedily, O LORD: my spirit faileth. (Psalms 143:4,7)

Serving Jesus does not immunize us against the harsh realities of life. We are people living in a sin-cursed world, and we will experience our share of sorrow, pain and anxiety. The difference between us and others is that we have access to a divine rest in the Lord Jesus Christ. We need to learn to gain access to this rest. While others are destroying themselves with extreme activities, we need to learn to relax in the Lord and wait patiently for Him.

My wife consistently tells me that my ministry improves after I have taken time out to rest. Relaxing from activity recharges my batteries. It is a form of being restored inwardly. I can stand and watch the waves of the ocean and feel emotional energy coursing through my being. As I take a walk in the mountains or sit in a flower garden, I find an inner renewal that is almost magical in nature.

How I wish I had understood this better in my youth. Now that I am past my seventieth year in life, I am learning to come into the presence of my Lord and say, "It's me again, relaxing in Your presence." This enables God to restore me again. Perhaps when resting in His restoration, I can enlarge my believing again.

8

Lord, It's Me, Believing Again

A Change of Faith

There is nothing more foundational to the Christian life than believing. While God's part in the plan of redemption is very complex and costly, our participation in that plan is almost simplistic. We are told:

> That if thou shalt confess with thy mouth the Lord Jesus, and shalt believe in thine heart that God hath raised him from the dead, thou shalt be saved. (Romans 10:9)

This confession is simply the vocalizing of our faith in the atoning work of Jesus at Calvary. The believing is inward, the confession is outward, but each is an activation of faith.

This *saving faith* is embryonic in nature. It is alive, it is effective and it is a gift of God, but it is very undeveloped. It needs time for gestation, and will need much tender care after its delivery. Like a baby, its maturity develops more rapidly after its first manifestation than before its birth. If faith is not allowed to mature in our lives, we will never progress beyond what baby faith can produce — conversion.

This maturing of faith can be seen in the parable of the Prodigal Son. As hunger caused him to change his mind about himself and his father's farm, he had sufficient faith in his father's integrity that he dared to return to offer himself as a servant. This was the extent of his faith before he got into the father's presence.

The warm reception given by the father stirred the son's faith to a higher level. The embrace and kiss told him that love still existed, and his faith rose to meet it. The robe and shoes let him know that his father was still the supplier of his needs, and faith rose to meet this. When the family ring was pressed onto his finger, the prodigal's faith in his father's restoration rose to new heights, for this ring represented his father's signature — it was his seal. Authority had been restored to the son. His faith increased as more facts were supplied.

We, too, develop in our faith as our heavenly Father unveils higher and higher relationships He has made available to us.

Paul rejoiced that the young Christians in Thessalonica continued to develop their faith. He told them:

> We are bound to thank God always for you, brethren, as it is meet, because that your faith groweth exceedingly, and the charity of every one of you all toward each other aboundeth. (2 Thessalonians 1:3)

They were doing something right, for their faith was growing, maturing and developing. Perhaps a strong clue can be found in Paul's first letter to them where he said:

> For this cause also thank we God without ceasing, because, when ye received the word of God which ye heard of us, ye received it not as the word of men, but as it is in truth, the word of God, which effectually worketh also in you that believe. (1 Thessalonians 2:13)

It was their embracing of the Word of God that caused their faith to grow, for "Faith cometh by hearing, and hearing by the word of God" (Romans 10:17). Time spent in God's presence and in God's Word is faith-producing and faith-maturing.

The Word of God is the food of faith, while believing is the fulfillment of faith. Both are necessary. We cannot effectively exercise under-developed faith. If we did, we would exhaust our faith. Faith is both forceful and fragile. We can develop it or destroy it. When Paul wrote to Timothy, his son in the faith, he spoke of people who had ruined their faith in four different ways:

1. A few made shipwreck of their faith by failing to maintain a good conscience. (See 1 Timothy 1:19.)
2. Some departed from the faith by giving heed to seducing spirits and doctrines of devils. (See 1 Timothy 4:1.)
3. Others erred in the faith by denying the future resurrection of the saints. (See 2 Timothy 2:18.)
4. Still others became reprobate in the faith by resisting and withstanding God's chosen leadership. (See 2 Timothy 3:8.)

These persons were not without faith, for, "God hath dealt to every man the measure of faith" (Romans 12:3). They simply mishandled that gift of God and lost it. Not one of us is without faith initially. We came into this world with a small measure of God's faith. Babies show that faith in their complete trust in their parents. Children are vulnerable because of their faith in adults, and without faith there would be no marriages.

Life would be difficult if not impossible without faith. We must have faith in our government, our financial institutions, and in ourselves if we are to live comfortably on this earth. How embarrassing it would be to have to examine the structure of a chair before sitting on it. We use it without examination because we have faith that the craftsman constructed it correctly.

When a person declares that he or she lacks faith, it is an admission that one of God's great giftings has been destroyed or lost. Fortunately, faith can be replenished by going to the source of faith, the Lord Jesus Christ. Jesus told His disciples, "Have faith in God" (Mark 11:22). The marginal reading is: "Have the faith *of* God." Faith is renewable, but that feat of renewal requires action on our part.

Faith is an integral part of God, and when He comes into our lives, faith comes with Him. In listing the fruits of the Spirit, the Apostle Paul placed faith as the seventh fruit to develop in the lives of believers. (See Galatians 5:22.) Some Bible versions translate this Greek word *pistis* as "faithfulness" or "steadfastness," but these are simply faith in action rather than in reserve. Throughout the New Testament, *pistis* is usually translated *faith*.

The New Testament also tells us that the third gift of the Holy Spirit is faith. (See 1 Corinthians 12:9.) So faith is initially a gift of God that increases both as a fruit and as a ministry gift of the Holy Spirit.

Increasing faith is not God's responsibility. He has given us, "All things that pertain unto life and godliness" (2 Peter 1:3). It is our responsibility to reach for these things and apply them to everyday living. Faith is increasable, but it doesn't expand automatically. It must be nourished and used. James urged us to use our faith without faltering. He wrote:

> Ask in faith, nothing wavering. For he that wavereth
> is like a wave of the sea driven with the wind and tossed.
> (James 1:6)

It is this fragility of a living faith that must grow to maturity that makes it imperative for us to come repeatedly to the giver of the faith — "The apostles said unto the Lord, Increase our faith" (Luke 17:5).

It's Me, Believing at a Higher Level

In one of my much earlier books, *Unfeigned Faith*, I make a distinction between faith and believing by pointing out that faith is a noun and believing is a verb. I suggest that faith is a divine energy while believing is the release of that energy. The faith is God's and He commits it to us. The believing is ours and God cannot do it for us. For the sake of this chapter, I chose to interchange the terms faith and believing, for faith is ineffective until we receive and release it.

In the pigpen, the Prodigal Son expressed faith that his father would make better provision for him than he could make for himself, but he was still starving. It was not until he activated that faith by the believing walk home that "knowing" became "receiving." Faith and believing must work together like a hand in a glove.

In Hebrews 11, the great faith chapter of the Bible, Abraham commands eight verses, which is more than anyone else. He is a magnificent example of the life of faith. While reading the Genesis account of his life of obedience, I saw at least seven separate steps in Abraham's believing faith:

1. Faith for conversion
2. Faith for sanctification
3. Faith for confrontation
4. Faith for multiplication
5. Faith for consecration
6. Faith for identification
7. Faith for perpetuation

God walked Abraham from the beginning levels of faith and trust to higher and higher levels. He enabled this man, whom He had chosen, to grow in his faith — very much as we help our children to grow in knowledge.

Abraham's first step of faith was responding to God's call to leave his homeland to follow God "unto a land that I will shew thee" (Genesis 12:1). He had nothing more than the command of God coupled with a promise to bless him and make of him a great nation, but when God speaks faith flows. Abraham chose to believe God, and he proved his faith by actually leaving Ur of Chaldea and made the pilgrimage to Canaan.

As is often the case, Abraham's faith became contagious. His father and Lot, his brother's son, and family came out with him as far as Haran where Terah, Abraham's father, died.

Abraham did not know where he was going, but he was beginning to know the God who was leading him. It is a fitting metaphor to help us understand our conversion experience. God calls us out of the world into a walk we do not understand. The path of divine righteousness is foreign to us, but we begin to know the One who is walking that path with us.

Just as we discover that conversion is followed by separation (the theologians call this sanctification), so Abraham discovered quite early that separation would be demanded of him. Lot felt that the time had come to separate from Abraham. He said that his herdsmen were constantly in strife with Abraham's herdsmen over pastureland. The gracious wording of the Scriptures puts it as follows:

> The land was not able to bear them, that they might dwell together: for their substance was great, so that they could not dwell together. (Genesis 13:6)

Although Abraham was tailed by Lot, who responded to a call given to his uncle instead of having his own call from God, this man of faith still offered Lot his choice of the territory. Lot selfishly chose all the plain of Jordan, leaving Abraham the mountainous regions. Lot got the watered land; Abraham got the wasteland.

Abraham had faith to believe that God would make good by allowing him to come out of this separation from Lot, and He did. Similarly, we need to mature in faith to let God separate us from everything that tags along and seeks to benefit by our consecration to God. God seems to permit people to do this for a season, but there comes a time when God produces division between us and anything that will hinder our further progression in faith.

Sanctification is always a double-edged sword. As used in the Scriptures, it means separation *from* and separation *unto*. Often God separates us from what seems to us good, helpful and even useful. God views things that are not of Him as bad, detrimental and useless weights that hinder our development. He wants us to believe Him enough to allow Him to separate us from these. In the imagery of the track star, we are encouraged:

> Seeing we also are compassed about with so great a cloud of witnesses, let us lay aside every weight, and the sin which doth so easily beset us, and let us run with patience the race that is set before us. (Hebrews 12:1)

Saving faith needs to mature into sanctifying faith. We originally let God remove sin from our lives. Now we need to trust Him as He removes everything that will hinder our maturing in His grace, even if it is a "Lot."

Years passed and God blessed both Lot and Abraham, but Lot found himself in the middle of a war. When Sodom and Gomorrah fell, Lot was captured and all his goods were taken as spoil. When Abraham heard this, he dared to arm his servants and pursue the kings that had captured him. With God's help, he soundly defeated the kings in battle. Lot was released and all his goods were restored to him.

Lot didn't deserve this rescue, nor was Abraham obligated to attempt it. He could easily have justified Lot's position and declared that it was none of Abraham's business. Instead, Abraham let his faith take still another step upward. He dared to believe that God would strengthen him in the battle to deliver his nephew from the enemy. Abraham had faith for confrontation with the enemy. Many generations later a disciple of Christ said:

> Be sober, be vigilant; because your adversary the devil, as a roaring lion, walketh about, seeking whom he may devour: Whom resist stedfast in the faith, knowing that the same afflictions are accomplished in your brethren that are in the world. (1 Peter 5:8-9)

There is an adversary who is seeking victims to devour. God asks us to rise in our faith levels and dare to resist — confront—him and defeat him. There are brothers and sisters whose faith has so diminished that they no longer have power over the enemy. God is still looking for Abrahams who will rise in faith to help deliver them in their hour of need. God has given to us a most forceful weapon against our enemy— faith. John wrote:

> For whatsoever is born of God overcometh the world: and this is the victory that overcometh the world, even our faith. (1 John 5:4)

Abraham was not a man of war, nor were his men trained in war, but he was a believing man whose faith could surmount his limitations. God, plus a believing person, outnumbers everyone.

Just a few years earlier, Abraham could not have done this. He was straining in faith to come out of his securities to walk with God in an unknown area. Then his faith was severely challenged when Lot walked out on him, leaving him with less than an ideal situation. But Abraham was learning that there is a progression in faith. We go "from faith to faith" (Romans 1:7).

There comes a time in our early Christian experience when we realize that our faith for conversion has matured to embrace faith for sanctification. We may have wept as things and people, who had formed our security blankets, were taken away from us, but our faith dared to believe, "The way of the LORD is strength to the upright" (Proverbs 10:29).

Having walked for a while in faith that embraced our conversion and sanctification, God dared to challenge us to a confrontation with our enemy. We doubted if our faith was up to it, but we discovered that:

> There hath no temptation taken you but such as is common to man: but God is faithful, who will not suffer you to be tempted above that ye are able; but will with the temptation also make a way to escape, that ye may be able to bear it. (1 Corinthians 10:13)

We discovered that God's imparted faith was up to the challenge if we would release it in a higher level of believing than we had used for our sanctification. That's why we often return to God's presence with the cry, "It's me, believing at a higher level, but help my unbelief."

It's Me, Believing for Greater Things

As our faith rises to greater levels of trust, God challenges us to believe for greater and greater things. Abraham returned from the battle that released Lot with a higher level of faith, for he had met and had fellowship with the king of Salem, Melchizedek—a theophanic manifestation of Jesus. Every time we meet Jesus at a higher level, our faith rises to higher levels with Him.

It was after this meeting that the Lord spoke to Abraham and promised him a son. When God's promise was not immediately fulfilled, Abraham tried to fulfill the promise for God by taking Sarah's maid as a concubine to procreate Ishmael. This work of his flesh that masqueraded as faith was a pain and problem to Abraham until the day of his death, and the conflict between Isaac and Ishmael continues to this day.

Whenever we try to do what God has said He would do, we end up with a work of our flesh that plagues us. Our belief needs to rise to the level of God's promises whether it seems possible for those promises to be fulfilled or not. It is not the measure of the promise, but the status of the one making the promise that we should focus on. If God said it, that settles it, for we live by "Every word that proceedeth out of the mouth of God" (Matthew 4:4). Anything we add or subtract from that word is to our detriment.

God mercifully reappeared to Abraham when he was ninety-nine years old and again promised him a son through whom nations would be formed. God promised progeny as abundant as the sand on the seashore or the stars in the heavens. Abraham found this difficult to believe and reminded God that his wife, Sarah, was ninety years old. When God merely reaffirmed His promise, "Abraham fell upon his face, and laughed" (Genesis 17:17). His faith was rejoicing.

God's renewed promise produced faith for multiplication. Abraham now believed that there would be a succession of men who would walk by faith. He realized that the promises of God would not cease with his death. He believed God's promise for a marvelous multiplication of his heirs.

God yearns to have our faith rise enough for us to believe that what has been done in us will multiply in succeeding generations. Throughout the Bible, God's covenant promises were made to a minimum of three generations — "you, your seed and your seed's seed." We must maintain faith for our children and grandchildren to walk in the covenants into which God has brought us.

At least twenty years later, God shocked Abraham by asking him to offer this son of promise as a living sacrifice on Mount Moriah. The twenty-second chapter of Genesis tells this well-known story. Although God ultimately did not allow Abraham to slay Isaac, Abraham did not know this until his knife was raised over his son who was bound on the crude altar of sacrifice. God provided a substitute ram in Isaac's place (a beautiful type of Christ) and revealed Himself as Jehovah-Jireh, "the Lord will provide."

God did not seek a human sacrifice; He sought a complete consecration from Abraham. When God gives us the desires of our hearts, He often asks us to place them upon an altar of consecration — giving them back to Him. This takes a higher measure of faith than is required to receive these precious gifts in the first place. God yearns for us to grow up sufficiently enough that we can join Job in saying:

> Naked came I out of my mother's womb, and naked shall I return thither: the LORD gave, and the LORD hath taken away; blessed be the name of the LORD. (Job 1:21)

God has a right to repossess anything that He has given. He offers us faith to consecrate to Him everything we are and everything we possess — both material and spiritual.

Sarah was 127 years old when she died in Hebron in the land of Canaan. This put Abraham's faith to the test again. Rather than merely burying Sarah where his tent was pitched, Abraham purchased a cave from Ephron:

> And the field, and the cave that is therein, were made
> sure unto Abraham for a possession of a burying place
> by the sons of Heth. (Genesis 23:20)

Abraham had faith to identify with Sarah's death. He not only provided for her burial, but for his subsequent burial. He had faith to face the reality of his mortality.

We need faith realistic enough to face our mortality. Far too many Christians die without a will to direct the handling of their earthly goods or without any predetermined burial arrangements. Their bereaved families have to make these arrangements in the midst of their grief. Abraham had faith to look to his future internment.

There is a precious spiritual lesson to be seen in Abraham's identification with Sarah's death. We have been asked to identify with the death of Jesus at Calvary. Paul testified:

> I am crucified with Christ: nevertheless I live; yet
> not I, but Christ liveth in me: and the life which I now
> live in the flesh I live by the faith of the Son of God,
> who loved me, and gave himself for me. (Galatians 2:20)

Jesus not only died for us, He made it possible for us to die with Him. Mature believing allows us to:

> Reckon ye also yourselves to be dead indeed unto
> sin, but alive unto God through Jesus Christ our Lord.
> (Romans 6:11)

Our sinful nature does not need to be controlled; it needs to be crucified. Death, not discipline, is God's provision for what Paul calls "the carnal man." Faith allows us to bring that sinful nature to the cross by identification. To take this step of faith often causes us to return to Jesus and say, "Lord, it's me again, believing for greater things than ever before.

Help me to believe for multiplication, consecration and identification in my walk with You."

It's Me, Believing for Different Reasons

While faith is unchanging, except for its intensity, the object of our faith and the reasons for that faith are constantly changing. We initially believe out of need — it is believe or perish. Subsequently we find ourselves believing because of irrefutable evidence. Jesus told the Jewish leaders:

> Believe me that I am in the Father, and the Father in me: or else believe me for the very works' sake. (John 14:11)

We eventually learn to believe because of relationship. We believe not because of ourselves, but because of Him. The very nature of God infuses faith into our hearts.

It was when Abraham really came to grips with the eternal nature of God, versus his personal mortality, that he realized he would live on through Isaac. He sent his eldest servant, Eliezer, back to his home territory to seek a wife for Isaac. Abraham wanted his son to marry one of God's covenant people rather than a Canaanite woman. He wanted God's best for his son.

The story of the camel train laden with rich gifts and of Rebekah's willingness to water these camels is precious. The favor God granted Eliezer in finding this bride so quickly and Rebekah's quick acceptance of the proposal to marry Isaac is further evidence of the richness of Abraham's faith.

Abraham believed God for perpetuation of the family line and the fulfillment of the divine promises. So must we. It is a high level of faith to believe that after we have passed from the face of this earth, the work that God began in us will continue to flourish. Our faith can reach beyond the grave if

111

we have exercised it for the younger generation that we are training. We must provide for the spiritual maturity of those who will follow us.

Throughout his entire life, Abraham: "Believed in the LORD; and he counted it to him for righteousness" (Genesis 15:6). The longer he walked with God, the higher his level of faith became. He believed God for conversion, sanctification, confrontation, multiplication, consecration, identification and perpetuation. So can we. We cannot start at the top, but we can climb higher and higher. We can repeatedly come into God's presence announcing, "It's me, believing again." Like the Prodigal Son, we not only increase in faith, but we also increase in love.

9

Lord, It's Me,
Loving Again

A Change of Relationship

There is nothing in Christ's story about the Prodigal Son that indicates the son ever ceased loving his father, and there is much indication that the father certainly maintained a love for this son. Still, the act of self-will exercised by this young man put that love to the test, for long separation is not conducive to a healthy love flow. It is also likely that the wounds and abuse he had suffered caused him to stifle his feelings of love.

All the guilt, sense of failure and deep hurting the Prodigal Son brought home with him impeded his flow of love and reception of love. One can imagine him standing erect and unresponsive as the father first hugged and kissed him. "I don't deserve this," was probably his inner attitude.

As faith in his father's honesty began to grip his heart, this returned runaway found himself able to receive some of the father's love, and this aroused his long dormant love. He had to believe in his father and in himself before he could respond to love.

Faith is as vital an ingredient of love as flour is to a cake. Nothing can take its place. It is not only a necessary ingredient, it is a major a component. Where faith is absent, love will fail.

In a healthy marriage, the more each partner believes in the other, the deeper his or her love grows. The initial love that brought the couple together may well have been founded on hope, but as hope matured into faith, love flourished. This triad is so interrelated that Paul placed it as the lasting force in life. He wrote:

> And now abideth faith, hope, charity, these three; but the greatest of these is charity. (1 Corinthians 13:13)

This interaction of faith and love is as real in our relationship with God as it is in our relationship with one another. As faith enlarges, our capacity to love increases. The New Testament connects faith and love in the same verse at least thirteen times. Perhaps the most outstanding example of this pairing comes from the pen of Paul:

> That Christ may dwell in your hearts by faith; that ye, being rooted and grounded in love, May be able to comprehend with all saints what is the breadth, and length, and depth, and height; And to know the love of Christ, which passeth knowledge, that ye might be filled with all the fulness of God. (Ephesians 3:17-19)

Paul was convinced that believing faith enthrones Christ in our lives, making it possible for us to be firmly established in divine love. With such a foundation, we should be able to mature with other saints to understand the dimensions of God's love and to know experientially a measure of this love that goes far beyond human comprehension. His prayer was that we "be filled with all the fulness of God." This is high-level praying, but Paul based it on the active faith in the lives of the saints. We can often answer our own prayers for more love by increasing the level of our trust in Christ.

114

It was this same Apostle who so paired faith and love as to call them the Christian's breastplate:

> But let us, who are of the day, be sober, putting on the breastplate of faith and love; and for an helmet, the hope of salvation. (1 Thessalonians 5:8).

Paul felt that these two should develop equally like the two breasts of the human body. Our normal progression in this development is from hoping to believing to trusting to loving.

God puts faith and love in symmetric balance for our protection because love makes us extremely vulnerable. No one can hurt us more deeply or more quickly than ones we love intensely. We must trust before we dare to love. If that trust is seriously violated, our love is threatened, and it often retreats behind defensive walls. It is not by accident that John wrote:

> If a man say, I love God, and hateth his brother, he is a liar: for he that loveth not his brother whom he hath seen, how can he love God whom he hath not seen. (1 John 4:20).

Some see this verse as a law of God, but I view it as an explanation our Creator shares with us. God knows that He created us with but one set of emotions. Both the soul and the spirit play upon them. The defensive walls we build to prevent other people from further wounding our hearts also prevent our love from flowing out to our brothers and sisters. These same protective barriers keep us from giving or receiving God's love.

If we choose to live in a bottle to protect our emotions, we must learn to live in a loveless environment, for we will be unable to give or receive love from God or another person.

In seeking to spare ourselves pain, we have denied ourselves pleasure. What price safety!

Often after a season of such isolation, we realize that it is better to give and receive love, even if it makes us vulnerable to wounds, than to live a loveless existence. That is when we come into the presence of God and happily announce, "Lord, it's me, loving again!"

It's Me, Receiving Your Love

The Prodigal Son returned home anticipating an opportunity to become a hired servant. That is all he asked of his father, but this request was never granted. Instead the father lavished love on the son. It took the son awhile to comprehend what was happening, but when he sensed that it was a genuine display of love, he received and responded joyfully to it, though he knew he did not deserve it.

Each of us is a prodigal who, upon returning home, has experienced a similar outpouring of God's love. This was, of course, completely unmerited and unexpected. We came to God in our sinful state, pleading for His mercy, but we found that Jude was accurate in saying that mercy comes coupled with peace and love. He wrote:

> Mercy unto you, and peace and love, be multiplied. (Jude 1:2)

The entire divine plan of restoration flows in a channel of God's love. Just as the father of the Prodigal Son was under no obligation to restore the boy to the privileges of a son, so God is not obligated to restore us. He purposed to redeem us out of a love motivation, He provided that redemption because of His love, and He purchased our redemption with His demonstrated love at Calvary. Little wonder, then, that John exclaimed:

Behold, what manner of love the Father hath
bestowed upon us, that we should be called the sons of
God. (1 John 3:1)

Receiving God's love is a learned experience. There was
little or nothing in our background to prepare us for such an
exhibition of love. We do not understand it, and probably
never will, but we learn to accept and respond to it.

Perhaps our greatest surprise is that God's love is a
progressive experience. He does not love us back into the
family and then ignore us. He continually extends His love
to us. Initially we feel awkward in this unending flow, but
eventually we begin to comprehend the truth that David sang
so long ago:

Blessed be the Lord, who daily loadeth us with
benefits, even the God of our salvation. Selah. (Psalms
68:19)

As we learn to bask in God's eternal love, we often
become so accustomed to it that we mistakenly assume we
can produce it. Love is part of the essential nature of God.
The four New Testament definitions of God (God is love,
God is light, God is holy, God is a consuming fire) are all
energies. Each of these definitions could properly be followed
with: [and you are not!] — "God is love [and you are not!]."

Only God is light, He alone is truly holy, and God
exclusively is love. If any of these spiritual energies flow in
us, we receive them from Him.

If love is part of the essential nature of God, it is not part
of the essential nature of persons, for God is unlike any other.
If we can produce love, then we can produce God. Any god
we can create is unneeded, for the created is always less than
the creator. In his brilliant epistle to the church at Rome, Paul
wrote:

117

> The love of God is shed abroad in our hearts by the
> Holy Ghost which is given unto us. (Romans 5:5)

Just as the consumer does not produce the electricity he
or she uses, so love is not produced by the user. Love always
has its origins in God, is transmitted to us by the Holy Spirit
and is used by us in our everyday living. We can receive love,
but we cannot generate it. We can share true love, but we
cannot store it. God is always its source; we are only its
objects. John, the Apostle of love, taught us:

> Love is of God; and every one that loveth is born of
> God, and knoweth God. (1 John 4:7)

Just as the air we breathe is renewable, but must be drawn
into the lungs regularly, so God's love is renewable, but we
must appropriate it habitually. It is never sufficient to have
come to God for His love. We must now come to Him for a
fresh measure of that love. If we fail to do so, we will find
ourselves living loveless existences with fond memories of
days of love.

This is why maturing Christians find themselves returning
to God's presence to say, "Lord, it's me again, receiving Your
love." Like the child with arms outstretched to the parent, we
ask God to pick us up again, hug us, and share His love with
us once more. He not only does so, but He enjoys doing it.
He delights in feeling us respond to His love.

It's Me Again, Responding to Your Love

Our response to God's love is as meaningful to God as
His love is momentous to us. Few things in life frustrate us
more than to lack a receptive object for our love. Love is a
potent energy that needs to be released, but love cannot be
given unless it is received.

In likening the energy of God's love to electricity, we not

only recognize that He is the generating facility and we the consumers, but we face the reality that there must be transmission lines to get that energy from the source to the demand. This requires at least two lines — a positive and a negative. We do not order the amount of electricity we intend to use. We tie into an electrical transmission and use what we need and return the unused portion to its source. The theory of electricity is that it travels to the utility on the positive line, and the unused electricity returns on the negative, or ground wire. If something severs either of these lines, the flow of electricity ceases. This is why opening a switch turns off a light or disables an appliance. The opened switch breaks the electrical flow.

Similarly, love must have a source and a return line — a positive and negative flow. We receive love from an outside source, and we return some of it to that source. The Holy Spirit is God's positive line that transmits love to us, and our faith forms the ground wire that returns love back to its source in God.

This is just as true in the natural as in the spiritual. Even human affection needs a responsive object for it to flow. One of the pains of aging is the constant loss of love objects. We get separated from our children and consistently bury our friends. Our measure of love does not diminish, but the persons who are willing to accept and respond to our love become fewer and fewer. This may be one reason why a number of elderly people become so bitter. It is not so much that they lack the love of others as it is that they lack other people who will receive and respond to their love.

Many older persons personalize their pets in order to compensate for this lack. When Grandma lowers herself into her easy chair, Spot, her mixed-breed dog, playfully bounds onto her lap. As she strokes his head and talks to him, she releases some of her pent-up love. In return, Spot licks her hand while furiously wagging his tail in response to her affection. Spot is both a receiver of love and a responder to love, and those responses are fulfilling to Grandma.

Doesn't this picture God's relationship with us? God is inherently love. If our understanding of love is correct, He must have a responsive object to His love in order for it to be complete. The Scriptures indicate that Lucifer, the highest of God's created beings in heaven, was once the object of God's love. He received this love, dispersed it among the angels and gathered their responses to return that love to God.

The fourteenth chapter of Isaiah says that Lucifer became proud and eventually revolted against God; thinking that he could replace God as the source of love. When Michael and his angels cast Lucifer out of heaven (see Revelation 12), it left God without a responsive love object, and the energy of divine love could not flow.

It is obvious that Adam and Eve were created to become God's love objects. That the arrangement was satisfactory to God seems equally apparent. This new creation did not have the majesty or ability of Lucifer, but because he and she possessed inherent powers of procreation, God would always have a plural object to receive and respond to divine love.

Lucifer, known on earth as Satan, was displeased to see God so completely fulfilled in this replacement object of the divine love, so he entered the Garden as a tempter and succeeded in cutting the return line of divine love flow. It is unlikely that Satan had any direct animosity toward Adam. His consistent aspiration has been to replace God. He has no desire to stoop low enough to replace man.

The work of the devil in the Garden of Eden was not to destroy Adam and Eve, but to disrupt the flow of divine love to and through them. He knew that such a flow was regenerative to God and Satan wants God to flounder; not flourish. Because he got all his training in heaven, Satan was wise enough to know that he could not disrupt the positive flow from God, so he worked on the return line. Adam's deliberate disobedience to God's Word disrupted the flow of God's love as certainly as an open switch turns off the lights.

The results of this were painful enough for Adam and Eve, but they were far more painful to Jehovah. Again the flow of divine love was halted. God's love was frustrated because it could not flow. But this action did not catch God by surprise. The Lord had foreseen this act of rebellion and had prepared for it before the foundations of the world were laid. He entered the Garden, slew a substitute sacrifice for Adam and Eve and repaired the broken line. It is unlikely that Adam understood that this slain animal was a type of the coming Lamb of God who would die as our substitute, but he did accept it as God's provision for restored fellowship of love. Adam did not need to understand this provision; he needed only to respond to it.

Because of the progressive revelation the Bible has shared with us, we have a better understanding of how God repaired this broken circuit. It is condensed beautifully in the words of Jesus:

> For God so loved the world, that he gave his only begotten Son, that whosoever believeth in him should not perish, but have everlasting life. (John 3:16)

God has done His part. Love is again flowing from His heart to our lives. The next step is ours. Since it is not possible to have a flow of love into our lives without a reciprocal flow back to God, responding to God's love involves more than merely receiving it. It requires returning it. It is beautiful and necessary for us to know that Jesus loves us, but it is equally imperative for us to assure God that we love Him with His own love.

I keep a music box on my desk top that plays "Yes, Jesus Loves Me" when I lift the lid. I raise that lid frequently when I am in my study, for I need to be reminded that Jesus does, indeed, love me. I have found this musical reminder to be far more valuable if, when the music stops, I add, "Yes, I love Jesus. I'm glad to tell Him so." I have been made aware of His love for me, and I have made Him aware of my love for Him. This seems to complete the circuit.

It would be impossible to remind God of our love for Him too frequently. It is vital that we learn to communicate to Him: "It's me again, responding to Your love." We receive His love, absorb and use all we need and return the unused portion back to Him. But there is still another cry that wells up in our hearts when God's love is flowing. We find ourselves expressing God's love to those around us.

It's Me Again, Releasing Your Love to Others

It is God's love that reaches men and women, but most people do not have a direct contact with the Lord. God has purposed that those of us who have learned to receive divine love should leak some of it onto others. We are not only witnesses of the power of God's love, we are demonstrators of it. Like the smiling young lady in the supermarket who offers a free taste of a new product, we give free samples of God's love to anyone who will accept it. Jesus actually gave a command when He said:

> A new commandment I give unto you, That ye love one another; as I have loved you, that ye also love one another . . . This is my commandment, That ye love one another, as I have loved you . . . These things I command you, that ye love one another. (John 13:34; 15:12,17)

That we must love one another with His love is self-evident, for we have no other source of true love except for God's love. When we share God's love with "one or another," they get a free sample of what God is like. It gives them a chance to "taste and see that the Lord is good" (Psalms 34:8). It costs us nothing to share this love, for it is all excess love that we would have returned heavenward anyway.

Releasing the love of God isn't as difficult as some have made us think. True evangelism — attracting people to Jesus — isn't so much the reciting of a series of Scripture verses as it is a releasing of God's love to the unloved, the wounded, the distressed and the oppressed.

When He was in His hometown synagogue, Jesus was invited to share something about Himself. He chose to read a passage from Isaiah. Calling for the second scroll of this book, He unrolled it until He found the portion that read:

> The spirit of the Lord GOD is upon me; because the LORD hath anointed me to preach good tidings unto the meek; he hath sent me to bind up the brokenhearted, to proclaim liberty to the captives, and the opening of the prison to them that are bound. (Isaiah 61:1, quoted in Luke 4:18)

Jesus told the people in the synagogue that this passage was fulfilled that very day. He was sharing the Father's love to the meek, the broken-hearted, the captives and those bound by sin, self and Satan. Later Jesus told His disciples and us:

> Verily, verily, I say unto you, He that believeth on me, the works that I do shall he do also; and greater works than these shall he do; because I go unto my Father. (John 14:12)

Jesus shared the Father's love and we are to share that same love. Sometimes we do this with a smile or a kind word. Often it is with a helping hand or shared provisions. Perhaps a sermon or a song becomes the medium that imparts God's love. On occasion I have seen people break into tears when

I smilingly said, "Jesus loves you." We seldom know what channel others are tuned to, so we must broadcast God's love on every channel available to us.

Sometimes we Christians interpret Christ's command to love one another as loving only the brothers and sisters in God's family. One wonders how we can get to be so exclusive when we are asked to pattern our lives after Jesus, and He and His Father "so loved the world" (John 3:16). We will have all eternity to express our love to the saints, but we are limited to our time on earth to express our love to the "unsaintly."

Far from picking and choosing those to whom we will let God's love flow, Jesus urged us:

> Ye have heard that it hath been said, Thou shalt love thy neighbour, and hate thine enemy. But I say unto you, Love your enemies, bless them that curse you, do good to them that hate you, and pray for them which despitefully use you, and persecute you; That ye may be the children of your Father which is in heaven: for he maketh his sun to rise on the evil and on the good, and sendeth rain on the just and on the unjust. (Matthew 5:43-45)

We cannot consistently do this out of mere discipline. It demands the impulse of divine love, for it goes against the grain of our human spirits, and it seems to violate common sense. Fortunately, the very love we seek to manifest becomes the motivation for the imparting of it.

Paul said, "The love of Christ constraineth us" (2 Corinthians 5:14). Saunders translates this phrase, "The love of Christ overmasters me, lifts me up and carries me along like an avalanche." The same divine love that transformed the lives of the messengers becomes our message and our motivation for demonstrating the message to friend and foe alike.

Far too many of us have thrilled at the transforming power of God's love without being willing to share it with others. As we mature in Christ, we rise above such self-centeredness and realize that what has been imparted to us is a basic need in every life. As increasing measures of divine love work in our spiritual natures, we can joyfully say to others, "Such as I have give I thee" (Acts 3:6).

It is evidence of great maturity to approach God and say, "Lord, it's me again, releasing Your love to others." This seems to be what the Prodigal Son did. After allowing his father's expressed love to rekindle his own dormant love, he began to release it to others. First, he obviously responded lovingly to his father. Then while at the banquet, he released his love to the servants who once had seemed so beneath him. Dignity and position have a way of disappearing when love is flowing. The privilege of sonship was lost in the glorious rejoicing of being back in the love of the family.

Perhaps nothing can bring us into rejoicing more rapidly than a flow of love. The Prodigal Son had known the emotional exhilaration of revelry, but it never produced true rejoicing. Only loving relationships can produce this.

10

Lord, It's Me, Rejoicing Again

A Change of Emotion

In the imagery of a young maiden being brought to the king to become his queen, the Psalmist speaks of her coming arrayed in beautiful garments with her companions and then says:

> With gladness and rejoicing shall they be brought:
> they shall enter into the king's palace. (Psalms 45:15)

This is what happened to the Prodigal Son. As he responded to his father's love, he was not only dressed in the finest robe available, but he was brought to a banquet for a time of great rejoicing. His hope in life had been restored. Paul taught the believers in Rome that we should:

> Let love be without dissimulation. . . . Be kindly affectioned one to another with brotherly love . . . Rejoicing in hope. (Romans 12:9,10,12)

We can rejoice when hope is restored, and a rejoicing spirit will restore tranquility. God is far less interested in having us remonstrate with Him than He is in having us rejoice in Him.

Wise King Solomon, after tasting just about everything that life could offer him, summarized his foundational philosophy of life by saying:

> Wherefore I perceive that there is nothing better, than that a man should rejoice in his own works; for that is his portion: for who shall bring him to see what shall be after him? . . . Rejoice, O young man, in thy youth; and let thy heart cheer thee in the days of thy youth, and walk in the ways of thine heart, and in the sight of thine eyes: but know thou, that for all these things God will bring thee into judgment. (Ecclesiastes 3:22; 11:9)

His ultra-simplistic summary was: *rejoice!* Solomon was aware of the shortness of life and the futility of constantly seeking the unobtainable. He urged us mere mortals to learn to rejoice in all things. He may have learned this philosophy from his father, for early in the Psalter, we hear David singing:

> But let all those that put their trust in thee rejoice: let them ever shout for joy, because thou defendest them: let them also that love thy name be joyful in thee . . . And my soul shall be joyful in the LORD: it shall rejoice in his salvation. (Psalms 5:11; 35:9)

The word "rejoice" occurs nearly 200 times in the Bible, and "rejoicing" can be found another twenty-eight times. We do ourselves a favor when we recognize that this is a command, for the Bible contains no suggestions. It is the will of God that we live rejoicing lives, for He created us to rejoice. Adam was made to enjoy the presence of God, and so are the recreated sons of the last Adam. (See 1 Corinthians 15:45.)

When God instituted the worship of the Tabernacle in the Wilderness, He did not design it to be a solemn, doleful ritual. He told Moses to instruct the people:

> And thou shalt rejoice before the LORD thy God, thou, and thy son, and thy daughter, and thy manservant, and thy maidservant, and the Levite that is within thy gates, and the stranger, and the fatherless, and the widow, that are among you, in the place which the LORD thy God hath chosen to place his name there. (Deuteronomy 16:11)

We recognize that there were times of confession of sin, and solemn moments when the priests slew the substitutionary sacrifice, but the purpose of gathering God's people unto Himself was to induce a spirit of rejoicing in them. It still is!

Worship sessions should never be so solemn that they could be mistaken for a funeral ceremony, nor should serving God produce joyless living. Jesus said:

> The thief cometh not, but for to steal, and to kill, and to destroy: I am come that they might have life, and that they might have it more abundantly. (John 10:10)

Jesus came, died, arose and ascended — not merely to give us spiritual life, but He came that we might enjoy an abundant life. This is life lived to the fullest extent. Abundant life means far more than material possessions. It speaks of full enjoyment. It is a rejoicing life, whatever it brings.

The theme of Christian living should be: **rejoice!** Our sins have been forgiven; rejoice! Christ rose from the dead; rejoice! Jesus is seated on the throne at the right hand of the Father in heaven; rejoice! Father God is still in control of all things; rejoice! We should stop taking ourselves so seriously and start rejoicing in the glorious God who has provided for us so abundantly.

Unwilling to learn from Solomon's experience and wisdom, some people never learn to seize the present moment and enjoy it. They are always looking to an unpredictable future. Far too many parents eagerly look forward to enjoying life when their children are mature and gone, while failing to enjoy the children in their lives at the present. Similarly, some Christians endure the present while anticipating the future. They have no present joy, but they anticipate an abundance of jubilation when they get to heaven. No one disputes the reality that heaven is a place of great joy, but we need not await our entrance to enjoy our Savior.

In fact, we need that joy in our present moments if we expect to arrive in heaven in the future. God's joy is an undergirding strength. When the Law was read and explained to the returned captives in the rebuilt city of Jerusalem, Nehemiah told them:

> Go your way, eat the fat, and drink the sweet, and send portions unto them for whom nothing is prepared: for this day is holy unto our Lord: neither be ye sorry; for the joy of the LORD is your strength. (Nehemiah 8:10)

Nehemiah didn't want them to continue weeping over their sin of breaking the Law. He assured them of God's forgiveness. Then he urged them to take the joy of the Lord with them as the needed strength to obey what they had just learned. He felt that they needed the strength of that joy more in their daily activities than in their public worship.

In the midst of daily activity, Christ's joy becomes a glorious source of strength for us. It also becomes a strong motivating force for our continued Christian living. The Bible challenges us:

> Looking unto Jesus the author and finisher of our faith; who for the joy that was set before him endured

the cross, despising the shame, and is set down at the
right hand of the throne of God. (Hebrews 12:2)

Divine joy was the motivating force in Christ's life, and
it should be in ours as well. We will do for joy what we will
never do for duty. The rejoicing heart is a willing heart.

It's Me, Rejoicing in Spite of My Circumstances

It would be completely dishonest of me to declare that I
can rejoice as readily in privation as I can rejoice in plenty.
My emotions are entirely different when in opening the daily
mail, I take an unexpected check out of the envelope than
when I find an unanticipated bill. Yet one mark of spiritual
maturity is to be able to rejoice in spite of our circumstances.

What a delight it is to read Paul's favorite praise word
throughout his letters — *rejoice!* He cried:

> Rejoice in the Lord alway: and again I say, Rejoice.
> (Philippians 4:4)

It is easy to overlook the fact that Paul was writing from
a crude Roman jail cell where he was chained day and night
to a Roman soldier. There was nothing in his circumstances
that would evoke rejoicing, but he had learned to rejoice in
the Lord in spite of his circumstances.

When I was young in the Lord, I tended to blame God
for every negative situation that came my way. My prayers
were basically "why" prayers. When I did not receive
definitive answers to my inquiries, I either introspectively
searched for something wrong in my life that had stirred God
to punish me, or I blamed God for unfairly making my life
miserable.

As I have matured in God, I have come to realize that
life is not all God or the devil. Life is filled with

131

circumstances that were not ordained by God or produced by the devil. Sometimes I am the cause of my own difficulties, and other times, they come just as the result of being in this sin-cursed world.

Happy are the Christians who stop seeking someone to blame for the negatives in life and who refuse to let these circumstances come between them and their God. Jesus told His disciples:

> It is impossible but that offences will come. (Luke 17:1)

Offenses, misunderstandings, failures and disappointments are part of living. Being a Christian does not immunize us from the negatives of life, but it does give us a divine companion to walk with us through those circumstances. Jesus has already walked through situations like these before, and He offers His wisdom to us as we walk through them now. When we recognize this, we can maintain our rejoicing in God in spite of our circumstances.

When we realize that God has a plan for our lives and that no power in heaven, earth or hell can prevent its fulfillment, we can rejoice in God in spite of our circumstances.

My ministry takes me from church to church and from country to country. Often, in preparation for a trip, I tell the Lord, "I don't know the circumstances of the congregation where I am going, but I know You. I rejoice that You will fit me into those circumstances in such a way as to bring glory to Your name and healing to Your people."

We were automatic rejoicers at the time of our conversions. As the excitement of conversion began to subside and the exercise of spiritual discipline set in, our rejoicing was often replaced with the melancholy of methodically living the Christian life. Somehow we forgot how the angels of heaven had rejoiced at our conversion, and we may never realize how Jesus rejoiced over us. Back in the days of Zephaniah, the Lord said:

> The Lord thy God in the midst of thee is mighty; he
> will save, he will rejoice over thee with joy; he will rest
> in his love, he will joy over thee with singing.
> (Zephaniah 3:17)

If God can rejoice over us, rest in His love for us and joy
over us with singing, surely we can "Rejoice in the Lord!"
Whether we look at His person, His works, His gifts or our
circumstances, we should be able—we must be able—to pray,
"Lord, it's me again, rejoicing!"

It's Me, Rejoicing in My Circumstances

This merciful, gracious and longsuffering God is also
"abundant in goodness and truth" (Exodus 34:6). God is a
good God who not only delights in doing good things, He
delights in giving good gifts to His children. James went so
far as to say:

> Every good gift and every perfect gift is from above,
> and cometh down from the Father of lights, with whom
> is no variableness, neither shadow of turning. (James
> 1:17)

God's gifts of grace, gifts of love and His gifts of the Spirit
have changed our circumstances in life greatly, so they are
consistent causes for our rejoicing. The prophet observed:

> They joy before thee according to the joy in harvest,
> and as men rejoice when they divide the spoil. (Isaiah 9:3)

God graciously gave me a wife who truly loves me. She
has been my supporter, companion, helper and lover for
nearly fifty years. Still, I rarely return home from a series of
special meetings without having her say, "Thank you for
everything you have provided for me." Often she goes on to

enumerate the house, car, kitchen appliances and bank account. She knows that these are provisions of my love for her, but she also wants me to know that she rejoices in them. She did not marry me for these things, for we thought we were headed for the mission field immediately after marriage. She accepts these provisions as bonuses in our marriage. The circumstances of our living together are comfortable, peaceful and pleasant. We rejoice together in these circumstances.

This would be a healthy attitude for us to take in our relationship with God also. He is the fundamental object of our rejoicing, but we also rejoice in all the bonuses He provides for us. God's redemption has great restoration in it. He not only "restoreth my soul" (Psalms 23:3), but He brings us into an enjoyment of life that the unconverted cannot experience.

The story of the Prodigal Son begins with good circumstances that the son did not appreciate. He wanted to create his own circumstances of life, so the father let him do so. We are all familiar with the despicable circumstances this son got himself into. We are always relieved that the story ends with restored circumstances. The father welcomed the son back into the fellowship of the family and the provision of the farm. This called for a celebration of feasting, singing and dancing. The father, servants and son were rejoicing that they could again share together in the good circumstances of life.

David knew adversity, but he also knew God's intervention into his life that brought him into a very good life. He wrote:

> The lines are fallen unto me in pleasant places; yea,
> I have a goodly heritage. (Psalms 16:6)

The American attitude is to reach for more of the "good life" with such drive that we fail to rejoice in the goodness of the life we are now experiencing. It is far too easy to transpose this into our Christian lives. Some Christians fail to enjoy their present level of fellowship with God because they deeply yearn to have something greater. Like the youngster who refuses to enjoy his or her childhood because of a deep desire to be an adult, Christians often by-pass the joys of the present while striving for imagined joys of the future. One of my wife's favorite verses is:

> This is the day which the LORD hath made; we will rejoice and be glad in it. (Psalms 118:24)

If we cannot rejoice in our today, we will never rejoice, for when tomorrow comes it will be today. God is pleased when we rejoice in the provision of the moment without losing faith in the future. It is proper for us to be content in the-here-and-now while making provisions to enter our futures. Paul testified:

> I have learned, in whatsoever state I am, therewith to be content. (Philippians 4:11).

He also wrote:

> Godliness with contentment is great gain. (1 Timothy 6:6)

In our early conversion experiences, we expected God's best for our lives. Unfortunately, we defined "best" as possessions, positions and power. We lived with dreams of spiritual grandeur and we expected to become one of God's mighty men or women. In retrospect we realized that most of our praying was a pleading with God to apply His Word and His power to help us find the American dream. Now it is embarrassing to remember the foolish vows we made to

God as we sought to bribe Him into fulfilling our will.

Instead of meeting the promises of His Word the way we interpreted them, God ignored our pleas, discounted our vows as the immature babblings of a baby, and accepted responsibility for our lives. He surrounded us with His love, filled us with His Spirit, and undergirded us with His grace. In this secure spiritual environment, we began to:

> Grow in grace, and in the knowledge of our Lord and Saviour Jesus Christ. (2 Peter 3:18)

Our spiritual growth also induced maturity in our every day lives. We began to relate as adults to both God and one another instead of as children. With this came a greater appreciation for life that caused us to return to the Father's presence to say, "Lord, it's me, rejoicing again."

It's Me, Rejoicing In My Creator

It is a pleasure to be around a person who rejoices in his or her marriage, but it is a double pleasure to fellowship with those who rejoice in their marriage partners. The first person finds pleasure in a state, while the others find their pleasure in a person.

While it is proper and scriptural to rejoice in our salvation, it is preferable to rejoice in the Savior. Because of the colossal change that God's salvation effected in our lives, it is natural that our initial rejoicing be rooted in this great gift of God. The prophet Isaiah, in the first division of his book, wrote:

> This is the LORD; we have waited for him, we will be glad and rejoice in his salvation. (Isaiah 25:9)

In the second division, and near the very end of his book, the more mature prophet said:

> I will greatly rejoice in the LORD, my soul shall be joyful in my God; for he hath clothed me with the garments of salvation. (Isaiah 61:10)

What had originally been the cause of the prophet's rejoicing became a divinely provided covering, not too unlike the prodigal's robe and shoes. This garment of salvation enabled the prophet to rejoice in the provider rather than in His provision.

As we mature in Christian living, our reason for rejoicing shifts more and more from the benefits we have received from God to God Himself. We come to realize that our relationship with Him is far more valuable than anything we could ever receive from Him. The song in our spirits becomes:

> The LORD, the LORD God, merciful and gracious, longsuffering, and abundant in goodness and truth. (Exodus 34:6)

The above verse is God's self-description to Moses on Mount Sinai. He is Jehovah-Yahweh—merciful in His nature. When we were first saved, we had a limited understanding of God's mercy. We were completely overwhelmed by His forgiveness. It is after we have walked in fellowship with Him for a season that we began to appreciate His great mercy. God had earlier spoken of Himself as:

> Shewing mercy unto thousands of them that love me, and keep my commandments. (Exodus 20:6)

The more we try to keep those commandments, the more we realize our inability to obey God's Word without the work of the indwelling Holy Spirit. In our initial failures, we expected divine judgement, but, instead, we received God's mercy. How we rejoice that the very throne upon which God is seated is called "the mercy seat" (Leviticus 16:2).

God also explained His essential nature to Moses as gracious. God is grace as surely as "God is love" (1 John 4:16). When God extends grace to His children, He is extending a portion of His very nature. The Psalmist sang:

> For the LORD God is a sun and shield: the LORD will give grace and glory: no good thing will he withhold from them that walk uprightly. (Psalms 84:11)

Grace is not just a New Testament doctrine that stands next to the righteous demands of the Old Testament law. Grace is revealed in the beginning of God's Book. We read:

> Noah found grace in the eyes of the LORD. (Genesis 6:8)

In the very midst of divine judgment, Noah found grace. How our hearts rejoice that when God pours out His judgment upon sin, we can come under the flow of His grace rather than endure the storm of His wrath.

This sharing of divine grace is a natural cause for our rejoicing. In our earlier Christian experience, we said that much of what we have received is because of God's grace, but over the years, as we walk in fellowship with the Lord, we change that to "all I have is because of the grace of God."

When we rejoice in our Creator, we must rejoice in His creation. How could a Christian stand on the rim of the Grand Canyon without rejoicing in God? When I journey through mountains or walk on the seashore, I marvel at God's great creation, and I often find a song of rejoicing bursting forth in my spirit. The Psalmist sang:

> For thou, LORD, hast made me glad through thy work: I will triumph in the works of thy hands. (Psalms 92:4)

It is not by accident that many young people, who abandoned the church before and during early marriage, return after the birth of their first child. It is hard to witness the continuing miracle of producing a child without being drawn to God. All His creation invokes rejoicing in the heart of one rightly related to Him.

Even looking in the mirror should cause us to rejoice. What a marvel we are. The amazing capacities God has entrusted to us inspired David to pick up his harp and sing:

> I will praise thee; for I am fearfully and wonderfully made: marvellous are thy works; and that my soul knoweth right well. (Psalms 139:14)

It is not that we have never rejoiced in God. It's just that as our understanding of God enlarges, our rejoicing in Him increases. The more we know Him, the more reasons we have for rejoicing in Him.

There is a side effect to maturing in our comprehension of God with its incumbent increase in rejoicing. The more we know about God, the more questions are raised in our minds. Even in our period of great rejoicing, we find ourselves questioning God again.

11

Lord, It's Me, Questioning Again

A Change of Trust

The story of the Prodigal Son doesn't end on a high note of victory. Although this son was completely restored by his father, the elder brother questioned the father's wisdom and actions. The older brother had earlier disagreed with his father over the request of his younger brother to receive his inheritance early. He viewed it as dangerous to the brother and damaging to the family business, for it cut their working capital by one-third and doubled the responsibilities for the older brother. "Why?" was his cry.

When the loving father later received and restored his Prodigal Son to full family relationship, the elder brother questioned the wisdom of this action. He did not feel what his father felt, nor did he think as his father thought. He had been convinced that his father was wrong in the first decision, but this present action was unthinkable.

Although the older son had worked faithfully for his father, it seems that he had little relationship with him, for he did not understand his thinking, his feelings, or his actions. Refusing to enter the banqueting house to join the celebration of the prodigal's return, this older son stood outside and argued with his father over what he had done with his own goods. Nothing had been taken from this brother. The father was simply sharing what was his, but jealousy made this son impudent enough to question his father's wisdom and actions. This display of pseudo-wisdom cost this son all the joy and celebration that the servants fully participated in.

Many of us are not far behind this elder brother. We question God's wisdom when He receives back into fellowship and restores to service the people whom we have rejected for "sinning." Our legalistic attitude would forever prohibit their return to the "farm," much less their becoming workers together with us and God again. We can give God a hundred reasons why this restoration is not in the best interest of His Church, but He merely reminds us that His ways and thoughts are immeasurably higher than ours.

Few things can strip us of the joy of the Lord and the celebration of His goodness faster than a feeling of superior knowledge and wisdom. When we explain to God how wrong He is, we cut ourselves from the joy of fellowship that lesser servants can enjoy. Since we think our ways are best, we will contend with God about the way He does things. We become contentious and lose the joy of being a follower of Christ when we try to be His leader.

If there is one thing above all others for which we should be ashamed, it is our questioning God. His self-revelation is that He is LORD — *Jehovah*. He is the self-existent One. He is essentially omnipotent, omnipresent, omniscient and eternal. He is the Creator; we are but His creatures. As the absolute Sovereign of everything and everyone in heaven and on earth, He gives the orders and we follow them. Yet, finite little created beings that we are, we dare to question Almighty God. This seemed to disturb Paul, for he asked:

> Nay but, O man, who art thou that repliest against God? Shall the thing formed say to him that formed it, Why hast thou made me thus? (Romans 9:20)

142

To ask God for wisdom is one thing, but to question His wisdom is another. God has not provided for us to challenge His wisdom, but He has promised to share His wisdom with us through the indwelling Holy Spirit. Paul lists the "word of wisdom" as one of the nine gifts of the Spirit that God has given to His Church. (See 1 Corinthians 12:8.) He also responds to requests for divine wisdom. James wrote:

> If any of you lack wisdom, let him ask of God, that giveth to all men liberally, and upbraideth not; and it shall be given him. (James 1:5)

Anyone who has touched a measure of the wisdom of God is quick to admit that God doesn't think as we think. God declared through the prophet:

> For my thoughts are not your thoughts, neither are your ways my ways, saith the LORD. For as the heavens are higher than the earth, so are my ways higher than your ways, and my thoughts than your thoughts. (Isaiah 55:8-9)

It would be hard to picture a greater diversity of thought patterns. It raises the question, "How high is up?"

It's Me Again, Questioning Your Work in Me

I have yet to meet the person who has never questioned God's gift of salvation, though his or her salvation was a miraculous work of divine grace that transformed their life. The initial ecstasy that accompanied the redemptive work fades as the pressures and trials of life proceed. The feeling that had been such an assurance had to be replaced with faith in God's Word.

Our personal salvation begins as a work of the heart rather than a work of the head. The New Testament affirms:

> For with the heart man believeth unto righteousness;
> and with the mouth confession is made unto salvation.
> (Romans 10:10)

The pressure of sin that brings us to Christ is emotional, and the initial experience of being released from sin is equally emotional. It is not that the mind is inactive, for, according to this passage in Romans, the heart and mouth work together. It is simply that feeling precedes the facts. Long before we understand God's plan of redemption, we find ourselves redeemed.

God did not provide for us to be saved through intellectual comprehension of truth. The Holy Spirit affirmed through the Apostle John that:

> In him was life; and the life was the light of men.
> (John 1:4)

Christ first introduces us to divine life, and then He brings us into divine light. He imparts life and then instructs that life. By invigorating the heart, the head is prepared for instruction.

Many of us were content to live in the experience of the heart. Life was different after we met Jesus, and that was all that mattered to us. We returned to Jesus from time to time for a renewing of His life, and we found this sufficient. There came a time or a set of circumstances, however, when our minds began to ask questions for which we lacked answers.

My parents often testified to the life-changing experience I had at the age of three. My conversion was as real as any adult in their congregation ever experienced. When I was in the first grade of school, God called me into the ministry, and I began to preach a year later. In my youth my whole life revolved around Jesus, His Word, and His ministry.

During my high school years I had a teacher, Mr. Burton Miller, who delighted in openly challenging my faith in the classroom. When I sought to answer his questions with a testimony of my experience, he made me an object of ridicule to my classmates. I was not unlearned in the Scriptures, but I was experience-oriented. My inability to communicate my faith began to arouse questions in me. Mr. Miller successfully challenged my faith, for my mind had not yet caught up with my experience. I was never in danger of losing my faith, but I began to wonder about some things that I believed.

In my boyish pride, I did not bring my questions to my father, for he was also my pastor, and I was his youth director. I tried to sort out my confusions by myself, but I only succeeded in making myself miserable. About this time, my English teacher also began to challenge my faith in the classroom, for I wrote all my essays about my Christian experiences, which opened the door for her challenges.

For several months, I found myself questioning my religious experiences, for I was not yet seasoned enough to find a scriptural basis for some of them. One night during my sophomore year, I refused to go to church with my parents. It was a first for all of us, but God gave my father sufficient wisdom not to force the issue. The first hour of being home alone during church night was one of the most miserable hours of my life. I paced the floor wrestling with my doubts and unanswered questions. I dared to cry aloud: "God, I don't even know if You are real. Am I wrong? Are my teachers right?"

In the pain of this questioning, I well remember dropping to my knees, lying across the front room couch and crying out to God in a way I had not prayed for several months. Tears flowed like a gentle spring rain, as God bathed me in His divine presence. God did not speak directly to me then. He just hugged me and made me aware of His great love for me.

In that fresh encounter with Christ, every doubt and question in my head submitted to the divine presence in my heart. I was in bed when my worried parents returned home from church. Seated on the couch where I had prayed, Dad began to express to Mother his deep concern about me. Feeling the wide wet spot where she was sitting, Mother said, "It's all right, Ep, Judson has prayed through."

And it was all right. I never again doubted what God had done in my life. In the days that followed I discovered something that happened to me that night. God opened my mind to understand the Word of God. What had been a sacred book to me became the living Word of a loving God. God enabled me to:

> Be ready always to give an answer to every man that asketh you a reason of the hope that is in you with meekness and fear. (1 Peter 3:15)

The open Bible became the foundation for my teaching ministry. I quickly switched from preaching to teaching as I shared with others the foundation for faith I had discovered in God's Word.

The longer I walk with God, the greater my sense of wonder becomes. Although I no longer question the reality of God's work in my life, I am amazed at the greatness of my Lord and the magnitude of His ways. I can often identify with the Magi who saw only an unusual star that filled them with wonder. By pursuing their wonder across the trackless deserts, they were led to Jesus. I, too, have learned to pursue my wonders until they bring me to Christ. There in His presence, I find the answers for which my heart had been searching.

All Christians have their questions, doubts and seasons of wondering about the truth of their experiences. This wondering is not sin — it isn't even wrong. It is necessary. Curiosity stimulates learning. We are very much like children exploring their world. First, we accept what we see or are told, but eventually, we must investigate and find out for ourselves. This experiential knowledge stays with us for a lifetime, while the facts we learned by listening or reading tend to slip away from us with the passage of time.

No, it is not sin to question our faith, for times of wondering come to each of us. What we accepted on the word of another when we were young Christians will someday be challenged in our minds as we gain maturity. These doubts can actually be healthy if we will admit them, for they can drive us to God and His Word to find a firm foundation for what we believe. Denying these doubts can be dangerous, for such denial will not lead us to seek an answer. Instead, we will dodge the questions and live with nagging doubts.

We Christians need to put our pride in our pockets and approach the Lord regularly with the cry, "Lord, it's me again, questioning Your work in my life and in the lives of others. Please help me to accept in faith what I cannot understand in fact."

It's Me Again, Questioning Your Work in Others

This honest questioning is merely the head wanting to catch up with the heart. The answer is not more education, although this is our standard approach to questioning. The real need in our lives is a fresh encounter with Jesus. The mind does not teach the heart about God; it is the heart that instructs the head. No one can better inform us about God than God Himself. When He illuminates His Word to our hearts, we learn more about Him in ten seconds than we would learn in ten college credits in systematic theology.

David did not expect his initial relationship with God to produce great understanding. He expected to have to learn the ways of the Lord. He wrote:

> Shew me thy ways, O LORD; teach me thy paths.
> Lead me in thy truth, and teach me: for thou art the God
> of my salvation; on thee do I wait all the day. (Psalms
> 25:4-5)

Obviously David expected a progressive work of revelation that would require a return to God's presence regularly.

Salvation may be an instant work of divine grace, but coming into an understanding and appreciation of this new way of life is progressive. We "grow in . . . knowledge of our Lord" (2 Pet. 3:18). Each new stage of maturity calls for new levels of knowledge and understanding. As long as we live, there will be more to learn.

As I said earlier in this book, I used to teach the organ. After explaining and then demonstrating on the keyboard the use of dominant ninths in downward progressions it was irritating to have the student ask, "Why?" I was prepared to answer a "When?" or a "How?", but "Why?" made no sense to me at all. Most of the "Why?" questions we address to God are totally out of order. Still, the little word *why* crops up in much of our praying. It also becomes the beginning of most of our complaints.

We are much like the elder brother in Christ's parable. When one of God's self-willed sons or daughters asks the Father's permission to take divine giftings away from home and use them for his or her selfish interests, a loud cry rises from earth toward heaven: "Why?" We don't understand why God doesn't prohibit such actions. Doesn't He know how much pain and suffering His refusal could prevent? He knows that this person is too immature to function profitably off the farm. If He knows so much more than we, why doesn't He do what we know is best?

The early Christian Church must have thought that God was making a serious mistake in calling Saul of Tarsus into an apostolic ministry. It is likely that several hundred "Why?" prayers ascended to the Throne of Grace. God did not answer them by prophecy, but He did let them discover in the life and ministry of Paul why God felt he was worth redeeming. By hindsight the Church now rejoices in God's choice. Had that early Church been able to see what we now see there would have been no "Why?" prayers.

God knows what He is doing, and He knows why He is doing it. David found this to be true. God directed Samuel to anoint David to be the King of Israel, but there was a season when David fled for his life from the reigning king. God sustained him in the wilderness and protected him from Saul. Interestingly, God never used the same method of defense twice. David had to depend upon God's wisdom in each new circumstance. Out of this experience David wrote:

> As for God, his way is perfect: the word of the LORD is tried: he is a buckler to all those that trust in him. (Psalms 18:30)

Hindsight always confirms that God's way was correct—perfect. We need to remind ourselves that God is eternal. He has no past or future. He lives in an eternal now. If what we perceive as past action was perfect, we dare to believe that God's actions will always be perfect — even His works in the lives of others.

We need to remember that God is less interested in retribution than He is in restoration. Jesus came as a Redeemer not as a referee. John testified of Jesus:

> For God sent not his Son into the world to condemn the world; but that the world through him might be saved. (John 3:17)

God has the right to reinstate the people of His choice into His family and service without having to negotiate with other members of the family about it.

149

Consistently we need to come into God's presence to pray, "Lord, it's me again, questioning Your ways in the lives of others. Please forgive me, and help me to remember that You love them as much as You love me. Please help me to join You in extending mercy instead of judgment."

It's Me, Questioning Your Work in General

Asking God "Why?" is totally unoriginal. Job, David, Asaph, Isaiah, Jeremiah and even Jesus all asked, "Why hast thou . . .?" Most of these questioners wanted to know why God had forsaken them. All of them lived to learn that God hadn't forsaken them, which proved the foolishness of the question. But, then, all questioning of God's ways is foolish.

Yet, children that we are, we continue to question God. As I travel across the United States, I have an increasing number of people who ask me, "Why is God giving such great revivals in third world nations when America seems so dry?"

Sometimes I answer them with the question: "Does God owe us an explanation?"

There are many rationalizations that seek to answer the question, but the question itself suggests an attitude that God must begin everything in America. We need to remember that Bethlehem and Calvary are in Israel, not North America!

Like the fans who are sitting in the bleachers and boo loudly to complain about the play the coach called for his football team, we Christians frequently question God's work in His world, and sometimes we vocalize our objections in a loud voice. Because we are here and He is there we feel that we understand better than He does. Our experiences in life should have taught us better than that, for the closer we are to the problem the narrower our perception becomes. It is viewing from a distance that gives the broad perspective.

We know deep in our spirits that God does all things

well, but we question much of God's actions or inactions in our emotions. It is common for the young couple to stand by the tiny coffin and sob, "Why did God let our baby die?" As we view the horrors inflicted upon fellow human beings in war we cry, "Why does God allow war?"

Somehow we hold God responsible for every negative incident that touches our lives. We wonder why He didn't prevent the automobile accident or keep the dam from breaking and spare thousands of lives. We hear ourselves saying, "If I were God, I would do things differently." We act as though we were puppets whose strings were held in the hand of Almighty God, but He has created us free moral agents with responsibility for our own lives. It is obvious that He can intervene since God has the power to do anything He chooses. That He cannot intervene without violating our individual rights seems less obvious to us. This is where prayer plays an important part. If we grant God permission to intrude in the issues of our lives, He may do so, and He may not. Only if we pray about a situation does God have this option open to Him. So often when we cry, "God, why didn't you help me?," He answers, "Why didn't you ask me to help?"

Like the soldier who questions the wisdom of capturing a specific military objective because he does not understand the battle strategy, we often question God's way of working in and through His Church.

Those of us who are involved in the work of Christ's Church on earth often question God's wisdom in placing the responsibility of spreading the Gospel throughout the world in the hands of the redeemed. Why didn't Jesus give this job to His angels? They are unhesitant in obedience, undefiled in character, and unlimited in power. Such persons are difficult to find in the Church on earth. The world would have heard the Gospel message within a week if Christ had commissioned angels to preach instead of asking mere mortals to do it. Why did God trust such an important message to us?

Many of us are unhappy with God's weather patterns. The local congregation prays for sunshine so their picnic will be undisturbed, but the farmers plead for rain so the crops will mature. We act as though God has weather control buttons on the arm of His throne.

If we were God, we would allow only the very old people to die, and they would always die painlessly in their sleep. Since we are not God, that is not the way it is. Death is only a breath away from any of us. We complain loudly at God as though He were a death angel strolling through humanity capriciously killing people on His walk. We tend to forget that death is a wage of sin, and that even though God has forgiven our sin, our bodies have not yet been redeemed. We will collect that wage, and we never know when our payday will arrive. God can intervene, but He is under no obligation to do so. He has provided for life after death, but He offers no immunity to death. Still, we blame Him for "letting him or her die."

Poor God! He gets blamed for so many things in which He is not involved. Even though He has the ability to do anything He wants, He is not obligated to do anything, any more than a rich individual is obligated to share his or her wealth with the poor. God fulfills His will as it is revealed in His Word, but He is under no obligation to fulfill our will. God does not exist for our pleasure. He created us for His own pleasure. The Psalmist declared:

> The LORD taketh pleasure in his people: he will beautify the meek with salvation. (Psalms 149:4)

We question so many things God seems to do. For instance, we ask:

1. Why does God permit such differences of interpretation of His Bible?
2. Why does God empower persons of weak character?
3. Why does God inflict the experiences of Job on some while giving the blessings of Abraham to others?
4. Why does God allow the devil such liberty and power?
5. Why does God permit the wicked to prosper while some of His saints live in poverty?

We would be wise to stop thinking that we can understand God. Maybe the attitude of David would be good for us. He wrote:

> Such knowledge is too wonderful for me; it is high,
> I cannot attain unto it. (Psalms 139:6)

God granted Job's wish to match his intellect with the mind of God. In three brief chapters, God asked Job a series of questions that scientists have spent their lifetimes probing without finding the answers. Perhaps we would do better to go back to playing with blocks instead of questioning the God of the universe about the way He orders this world.

It is not that God enjoys our ignorance. He repeatedly gives us wisdom and understanding through His Word. He explains His ways so we are able to discern them. Sacred historians have told us what God has done, gifted teachers seek to make His present ways plain to us and anointed prophets often give us a glimpse into what God is about to do. Still, any knowledge we receive is incomplete. We need to learn to walk in faith, embrace what we comprehend, and trust Almighty God to lead us into His very best, whether we grasp the ramifications of the route or not.

Small children who live in the security of being loved and cared for enjoy their parents without understanding them. Why, then, don't we just enjoy our relationship with God without being unduly disturbed by our inability to understand Him? Do we find it necessary to understand an automobile to enjoy using it? None of us needs an electrical engineering degree to enjoy colored television. Why then do we feel we must have a deep theological understanding of God to enjoy Him?

While questions from an honest heart are acceptable to God, a heart that habitually questions God's work and ways is apt to become a complaining heart, and this can lead to deep, deep trouble.

12

Lord, It's Me, Complaining Again

A Change in Understanding

It is easy to wonder if the relationship between the father and the elder brother of the Prodigal Son may have been strained even before the prodigal returned to the farm. We often neglect long-term relationships and allow them to deteriorate. It is probable that the son, who remained on the farm with the father, was now in charge of the whole operation, and his business may have separated him from close fellowship with his father.

All close relationships among people have their ups and downs. Even marriage fails to maintain a consistently high emotional plateau. The ecstasy of the courtship and the excitement of the wedding eventually level out to an emotional plane that is often based on confrontation. The couple discovers that keeping the promises of courtship is more difficult than anticipated, and merging two life-styles into one presents conflicts. Life has taught us that the excitable side of relationships often rides a roller coaster. When the emotional level is low, the complaint level is usually high.

Our relationship with Christ often becomes a similar scenario. The tremendous transformation of life that occurred at our conversion experience brought us a joy beyond our wildest imaginations. For months we lived in a brand-new world of celestial celebration. Like the newly engaged maiden who shows her ring to everyone, or the new father who proudly displays pictures of his child everywhere he goes, we brag on Jesus to anyone who will listen during the days of our early conversion experience. We want and expect this euphoria to last for a lifetime, but it doesn't.

As certainly as the young maiden's ring gets soiled in the work of the kitchen and the new baby demands attention twenty-four hours a day, our euphoric dreams dim as we settle into the near drudgery of making those dreams become a reality. The jubilation of joy is replaced with the juggling of the job with all the other activities life demands, and our complaints get louder and louder.

It is not that the Lord changed or that His benefits ceased. God is changeless and all His provisions endure into eternity. The Psalmist challenged us:

> O give thanks unto the LORD; for he is good: for his mercy endureth for ever. (Psalms 136:1)

Each of the twenty-six verses of this Psalm end with: "For his mercy endureth for ever." Everything in our relationship with God remains constant from His perspective. It is we who have unrealistic expectations that cause us to complain when they are not met as rapidly as we feel they should be met.

Many Christians cannot accept their humanity after being saved. The awakening of their spirits introduces them to such a new realm of life that they try to remain perpetually in this spiritual realm — denying that they live in a very earthly body and an extremely unspiritual world. When the pressures of life force them to come out of the clouds and place their feet on the earth, they have an extreme emotional letdown, and they become gripers. Nothing pleases them and they quickly go to God with their supposed grievances.

We should not allow this to happen to us. Just as the married couple must balance the thrill of a shared candlelight dinner with the truth of monthly mortgage payments, we need to be able to adapt from the ecstasy of eternal life to the ordinary occupation of everyday living. Christ did not redeem us for short-term pleasure. He restored us unto Himself for a lifetime of personal relationship. Some of this will be in our eternal spirits, but most of it will be in what we often call our "natural" lives.

Jesus told a parable contrasting a faithful and a slovenly servant. In it He said:

> His lord said unto him, Well done, thou good and faithful servant: thou hast been faithful over a few things, I will make thee ruler over many things: enter thou into the joy of thy lord. (Matthew 25:21)

The faithful servant was not removed from servile duty; he was promised joy while living a servant's life. The joy offered to him was not the joy of servanthood. He was invited into the joy of his master. He was not promoted to the head of the complaint department; he became the chief in the service department.

It's Me, Complaining about Prodigal Sons

In working to rescue fallen ministers and restore them to the ministry, I have found it easier to rehabilitate them than to get Christians to accept them as restored to the grace of God.

Historically, the Church has had problems with accepting forgiven prodigal sons. For the unholy to be restored to our level seems to negate the price we have paid for holiness.

Those who have not departed from the Father's house can testify with the sons of Korah:

> For a day in thy courts is better than a thousand. I had rather be a doorkeeper in the house of my God, than to dwell in the tents of wickedness. (Psalms 84:10)

Still, those who never wander have no basis for pride. Instead, they should cry:

> With my whole heart have I sought thee: O let me not wander from thy commandments (Psalms 119:10), for, We are kept by the power of God through faith unto salvation ready to be revealed in the last time. (1 Peter 1:5)

This position of humility and thanksgiving to God is not always the posture of Christians who remain consistently in the Father's house. The story of the Prodigal Son includes the incident of the older brother who reacted in anger at the treatment his brother received from the father. He overstated his brother's actions and then told his father:

> Lo, these many years do I serve thee, neither transgressed I at any time thy commandment: and yet thou never gavest me a kid, that I might make merry with my friends: But as soon as this thy son was come, which hath devoured thy living with harlots, thou hast killed for him the fatted calf. (Luke 15:29-30)

Jealousy causes many saints to resent the return of a wanderer. Their faithfulness and steadfastness to the commands of God have made them legalists who know little to nothing of the grace of God. They have been such faithful workers *for* God that they have almost forgotten the forgiving nature of this God. They have unwittingly become believers in works' righteousness. They are convinced that they maintain their salvation through their consistent religious works, and God's grace is unknown to them.

Through the years I have watched various ministers accept a position, either by election or appointment, to high religious posts and become elder brothers. They are proud of the office they hold and of their accomplishments and they frequently judge those under their dominion with harshness. They seem, somehow, to forget the depth of sin they were in when God found them, and they have very little time for anyone whose life is less holy than their's.

These men frequently die in their elder brother status. I have, however, observed some who, after stepping out of office, came in contact with real life again and often become great preachers of grace. They testify that they had become so busy in their work for God that they had lost contact with the God of their work.

The fields are, indeed, white unto harvest. While there is a shortage of laborers, all faithful elder brothers need to come to the table and sit with the Father in fellowship and relationship regularly. If we do not, we will become biased, exclusive and legalistic. From this position, we will resent anything the Father does for the laborers who abandoned the fields for the fun of the city. We will forget the father's response to the elder brother: "Son, thou art ever with me, and all that I have is thine" (Luke 15:31). God rewards righteous-ness, but He also extends grace and mercy to the unrighteous ones who repent and return.

When I pastored in southeastern Washington, I ran into a classic example of this elder-brother syndrome. A woman came to our church and pled with the congregation to join with her in prayer for her wayward husband. Each prayer meeting night she introduced us to another aspect of his escapades, as she again urged us to pray earnestly for his salvation.

After about a year, God mercifully answered these prayers and Arthur came to God in a very dynamic way. We were in a building program at the time and he became a key worker with us. He donated long hours of work and supervised all our cement work. Then he volunteered to work in our Sunday School. It was obvious to the entire church, and to the men with whom Arthur worked as a block layer that God had fully restored this backslidden husband.

To my bewilderment, Arthur's wife stopped attending church. No amount of visiting, pleading or praying for her could get her to come back. "I can't stand seeing my husband so accepted and working for God after all he has done to me," was the reason she gave. Once again she was complaining, but this time she was complaining that God had received and restored her prodigal husband.

I know, of course, that she had unforgiveness coupled with a loss of attention that her prayer requests had given her that year, but I also recognized the spirit of an elder brother. She was convinced that her husband did not deserve the grace that God bestowed upon him.

The tables were now turned and it was Arthur requesting prayer for his wife in the Thursday evening prayer meetings. Our congregation prayed for her just as faithfully as they had prayed for him. It took about two years before she returned to church and was reinstated to fresh fellowship with God. We were all amazed that when she returned, Arthur left. By now, he had embraced the spirit of the elder brother and felt that she did not deserve the grace God was extending to her. When I talked with him, I found a complaining spirit in him. He was complaining that God had received into fellowship his prodigal wife.

Prodigals get lost from fellowship with the Father, but elder brothers get lost from that same fellowship by becoming workers *for* God instead of being ". . . workers together *with* him." Little wonder, then, that Paul added:

> I beseech you also that ye receive not the grace of God
> in vain. (2 Corinthians 6:1)

Fellowship with God is never dependent upon what we have done. It is always contingent on what He has done.

It is beautiful when a prodigal returns to the Father's house, but we need to have the elder brother crying out in repentance: "Lord, it's me, complaining again. Restore me to Your grace as You have restored my brother."

It's Me, Complaining about Unanswered Prayer

It is often said that children live in a world of black and white. Things are either right or wrong — true or untrue. They know nothing about shades of gray. This is equally true of God's younger children. After our conversion, everything was simplistic to us. We saw our world divided between the dominion of God and the dominion of the devil. No one explained to us that the dominion of self was our greatest problem.

We brought that same mind-set to Christ's teaching about prayer. We embraced prayer as a magic lamp that needed only to be rubbed to release a genie to do our bidding. After all, Jesus did say:

> Therefore I say unto you, What things soever ye desire, when ye pray, believe that ye receive them, and ye shall have them. (Mark 11:24)

With this verse memorized, we approached prayer as children approach Santa Claus, except we were demanding rather than requesting. Amazingly, we often received immediate answers to our requests.

As we began to mature, the Holy Spirit impressed upon us that there are often conditions we must meet to get our prayers answered. He talked to us about faith, love, obedience and forgiveness. This stirred loud complaints in most of us. "How come the rules have been changed?" we asked. There had been no rule changes, of course. We were merely being forced to respond to the entire book of rules, not a favorite verse or two.

As a house guest, I sat in the front room reading a magazine as the three-year-old daughter sat on the carpet

playing with her doll. I was startled to hear a very com-
manding little voice call, "Mother, come here!" In a few
moments I heard this daughter stomp her little foot and
demand, "Mother, come here this instant!" It sounded like this
child was in charge of the home. When the mother did not
instantly appear, the little girl went into a flood of tears.

"What's the matter," the mother asked as she rushed into
the room?

"Where were you when I told you to come here?" the
daughter demanded.

Embarrassed to have such a scene played in front of her
guest, the mother quickly rushed the child to her bedroom, as
I sat there applying this little drama to what I often see in the
churches I visit.

Just as this child was accustomed to an instant response
to her crying, young Christians get used to having God
respond almost immediately to their petitions. As they mature,
those cryings become demanding prayers as they stamp their
feet and command God to do their bidding.

There comes a time in our maturing relationships when
God takes us aside and explains that He is God, and we are
not. He is the Father; we are the children. He gives the orders;
we obey them. God doesn't even have to be "right." He is
God. There is no higher authority on earth or in heaven, and
we learn that we may petition God, but we have no authority
to command Him.

This is a frustrating time in our Christian experience. We
are considered too immature to cry for a bottle, but we have
not matured sufficiently to know how to ask for our needs to
be met. We often react to our frustration with loud complaints.
We declare that God doesn't answer prayer as He has
promised to do. We tell others that God has abandoned us.

The truth is that God is teaching us that *yes!* is not His
only answer to prayer. Sometimes God says *no!*, and that is
an answer. My book, *What Is There About NO You Do Not
Understand?* (Sharon Publications, England) has twenty

chapters explaining the value of a *no* answer to prayer. God answers prayer according to His wisdom, not according to the intensity of our praying. It is not evidence of a lack of faith to receive a *no* answer from God. Faith enables us to touch God with prayer, but it does not determine the answer we will receive from Him.

Sometimes God says, "Later." He will grant our petition after we have matured sufficiently to handle that answer without endangering ourselves and others. Just as no father will give a pocket knife to a two-year-old son, God will not give gifts that are too far beyond our maturity levels.

Perhaps God's favorite way of answering prayer is by saying: "I will if you will." He expects us to meet the conditions before He will meet the promise. Few Bible promises are unconditional. Most of them are a form of:

> If my people, which are called by my name, shall humble themselves, and pray, and seek my face, and turn from their wicked ways; then will I hear from heaven, and will forgive their sin, and will heal their land. (2 Chronicles 7:14)

God will hear, forgive and heal when we meet the four conditions of humbling, praying, seeking, and turning.

All too frequently, we form a complaint department about unanswered prayer instead of learning how to pray more mature prayers. God is never seeking a loophole that will enable Him to bypass His Word. He delights in responding to our prayers, but He has committed Himself to our maturity. He dares not leave us as infants or pre-schoolers forever. We absolutely must learn to fill a responsible place in His family, and that begins by acknowledging that He is Lord of all — including us.

Perhaps our complaints about unanswered prayer would diminish if we would begin our days by praying, "Lord, what would You have me to do today?" instead of: "Lord, this is what I would have You to do today."

As we begin to realize that what we claim to be unanswered prayer is merely God answering differently than we dictated, we need to come to God in humble confession and say, "Lord, it's me complaining about unanswered prayer. Please help me to accept Your answers, and show me how to pray better prayers."

It's Me, Complaining about Life's Negatives

Learning to pray according to the will of God does not completely stop our complaining. We merely find something else to complain about. The human heart is like that. The word *complaint* occurs just nine times in nine separate verses in our Bible. It is not surprising that five of these verses are in the Book of Job, for this distressed man, with all of his patience, complained bitterly against the negative circumstances that overwhelmed him.

Because we have the advantage of chapter two of the Book of Job that explains to us how the whole episode was ordained of God, we tend to be critical of this early patriarch. Still, when we are undergoing similar testings, we are just as full of complaints as Job was. Somewhere in our early walk with God, we got spoiled. We assumed that life in the Spirit would be all positives and we ignored the purpose of the promise:

> But ye shall receive power, after that the Holy Ghost is come upon you: and ye shall be witnesses unto me both in Jerusalem, and in all Judaea, and in Samaria, and unto the uttermost part of the earth. (Acts 1:8)

Why do we need power if there is to be no opposition? How can we be witnesses to the "uttermost part of the earth" without suffering the hardships of going to those places? Paul admonished us:

> Thou therefore endure hardness, as a good soldier of Jesus Christ. (2 Timothy 2:3)

Paul wrote of some of the hardships he had to endure in the exercise of his ministry:

> Are they ministers of Christ? (I speak as a fool) I am more; in labours more abundant, in stripes above measure, in prisons more frequent, in deaths oft. Of the Jews five times received I forty stripes save one. Thrice was I beaten with rods, once was I stoned, thrice I suffered shipwreck, a night and a day I have been in the deep; In journeyings often, in perils of waters, in perils of robbers, in perils by mine own countrymen, in perils by the heathen, in perils in the city, in perils in the wilderness, in perils in the sea, in perils among false brethren; In weariness and painfulness, in watchings often, in hunger and thirst, in fastings often, in cold and nakedness. (2 Corinthians 11:23-27)

Paul was so certain that he was moving in the will of God that he didn't bother to complain about these things, although he complained three times about what he called "a thorn in the flesh." God's answer to this complaint was simply:

> My grace is sufficient for thee: for my strength is made perfect in weakness. Most gladly therefore will I rather glory in my infirmities, that the power of Christ may rest upon me. (2 Corinthians 12:9)

It is to be expected that God wishes He had more children with the same attitude as Paul. Most of us would have complained harshly if Paul's afflictions were heaped upon us. Job did. Even Hannah complained bitterly to God over her barrenness.

Our English translations of the Bible put the heading to a Psalm in italics before verse one, but I have discovered that translations into most other languages make that title the first verse of the Psalm. Because we rarely read the headings to the Psalms, we may easily overlook the purpose of a given Psalm. For instance, the heading to Psalm 102 states:

A Prayer of the afflicted, when he is overwhelmed, and poureth out his complaint before the LORD.

This is the perfect Psalm to read when we feel like complaining about our negative circumstances. It is easy for us to identify with the first ten verses. The Psalm does, however, have a turning point. The Psalmist says:

My days are like a shadow that declineth; and I am withered like grass. But thou, O LORD, shalt endure for ever; and thy remembrance unto all generations. (Psalms 102:11-12)

In seeing the contrast between our fleeting life and God's eternity, things start to get into perspective, and the Psalmist moves from complaints to praise. So should we.

The basic reason we complain so much about the negatives that come into our lives is that we are looking at ourselves instead of looking to Jesus. If we have His presence in the midst of these contrary circumstances in life, He will show us the way through them and make them work together for our good.

As we grow in maturity, we should learn to come before God in honest prayer and say, "Lord, it's me, complaining about life's negatives. Please help me to bless You for all the positives You have shared with me, and show me how to walk in my present situation."

We are self-centered throughout most of our lives. Even our worship tends to focus on our feelings. It is likely that we will have but momentary seasons of rising above this during our earthly journey through time, but when we step out of the dimension of time into timeless eternity, we will enter into a much higher dimension of the Gospel and find worship to be totally focused on God.

13

Lord, It's Me, Worshiping Again

A Change of Response

When we hold God responsible for the negatives in our lives, we ask a lot of "Why?" questions, and our lives are filled with complaining. We become depressed as we habitually look inward. Looking outward causes us to be distressed, but when we look upward we can be at rest. Depressed and distressed people consistently look for someone to blame, and Christians tend to blame either the devil or God. The elder brother of the Prodigal Son blamed the father.

Christians need to look to God the Father as the cause of our rejoicing, not the cause of our problems. He is a good God, and He has purposed and provided good things for His children. His promise to us is:

> The LORD God is a sun and shield: the LORD will give grace and glory: no good thing will he withhold from them that walk uprightly. (Psalms 84:11)

The Christian who has developed the upward gaze will still have questions and amazement. The victorious saint brings his or her wonder to the place of worship. A song of degrees that the Israelites sang on their festive journeys to Jerusalem reads as follows:

> I will lift up mine eyes unto the hills, from whence cometh my help. My help cometh from the LORD, which made heaven and earth. He will not suffer thy foot to be moved: he that keepeth thee will not slumber. Behold, he that keepeth Israel shall neither slumber nor sleep. The LORD is thy keeper: the LORD is thy shade upon thy right hand. The sun shall not smite thee by day, nor the moon by night. The LORD shall preserve thee from all evil: he shall preserve thy soul. The LORD shall preserve thy going out and thy coming in from this time forth, and even for evermore. (Psalms 121:1-8)

Believers in our generation need to appropriate this confidence. Almighty God is in charge of things both in heaven and on earth. We are not creatures of whim who are subject to the winds of fate. We are the creation of God and objects of His loving care. As the sons of Asaph said in the above Psalm, God has set Himself as our helper, provider, protector and sustainer. There is no greater security than our Savior provides in Himself.

Children that we are, what we do not know far exceeds what we do know. We may not even know where we are going, but we know Who is leading us. Our inability to comprehend His way and His work, much less to understand His person, should never prevent us from worshiping Him. His very transcendence produces an awe and reverence that leads us to worship Him at higher levels than we understand Him. It is His person, not His performance, that inspires our worship.

If there was ever a "me again" person, it was the Prodigal Son of whom Jesus spoke. As we've seen, he fits every category we have explored together in this book. In his hungering state of ruin, he came home and asked to be hired as a servant. He had faith to return to find a job, but he was received with great joy as a son. He approached the father with repentance in his heart, but he was quickly ushered into the banquet room for a season of rejoicing. None of this became a reality for him until he diverted his attention away from his problem and focused his consideration on the father. When he told the father, "It's me again," he moved from his failures to his father's favor.

When we turn our gaze from the negatives in life to God's gracious provisions, it produces a thanksgiving in our hearts that when expressed toward God becomes praise and, perhaps, even ascends into worship. David cried:

> Thou hast turned for me my mourning into dancing: thou hast put off my sackcloth, and girded me with gladness; To the end that my glory may sing praise to thee, and not be silent. O LORD my God, I will give thanks unto thee for ever. (Psalms 30:11-12)

I'm Worshiping Again because I've Returned

It is self-evident that the Prodigal Son had not worshiped for a long time, for in his religious culture, worship was expressed through the Old Testament sacrifices and rituals that could be performed only in the Temple in Jerusalem. When he left the country, he cut himself off from this worship experience. Furthermore, worship does not spring from a person who has separated himself or herself from the father, family and friends. Worship often finds its highest expression in united responses with others.

When we depart "into a far country," we cease to worship, for worship is a response to God. There can be no worship if we lack God's presence. Many congregations of people, who once enjoyed God's nearness and responded to it in praise and worship, have departed from that presence and they have had to replace worship with ritual, service and program. Worship is no longer a part of their lives. The self-seeking that causes us to leave the Father's house also precludes any worship of the Father. We may maintain loving memories of Him, but there will be no loving responses to Him.

The Prodigal Son had close fellowship with his father when he was on the farm. They worked the fields together, ate their meals together as a family, and the evening was a time of family fellowship. These times of close relationship to one another made praise and worship a natural expression that flowed out of this association. These opportunities disappeared when the relationship was gone. Similarly, we cannot worship God in absentia.

The older brother charged his brother with wasting his inheritance on strangers and harlots, and we know that when everything was spent, he joined himself (became an indentured servant) to a citizen of another country. Much like Samson of old, this son preferred to fellowship with people outside the covenants of God.

We could wish that this desire died with these two men, but Christians of all ages have had to contend with this yearning. Far too many believers feel that the world offers more excitement than Christ does. They are willing to attend church on Sunday morning, but for the rest of the week, they prefer the fellowship of unbelievers. They want to walk as close to the world as possible without losing their salvation.

Today we see dedicated Christians marrying unsaved persons more and more frequently — joining themselves to citizens of another country. Paul warned believers:

> Be ye not unequally yoked together with unbelievers: for what fellowship hath righteousness with unrighteousness? and what communion hath light with darkness? (2 Corinthians 6:14)

The bonding of believers and unbelievers into close fellowship will deter worship of Jehovah. For the sake of fellowship, the righteous person will often set his or her righteousness aside to fellowship with the unrighteous. This cuts off worship instantly. Fellowship with God is substituted with friendship with the world and James warns us:

> Ye adulterers and adulteresses, know ye not that the friendship of the world is enmity with God? whosoever therefore will be a friend of the world is the enemy of God. (James 4:4)

Away from the farm and joined to strangers, the Prodigal Son discovered that when he no longer had anything to give to these strangers, they no longer wanted his presence. In desperation he ended up feeding pigs — an animal he had no experience with since they were an unclean animal to the Jews.

It was almost impossible for worship to ascend from this pigpen. The Prodigal Son was in no position to worship. David called for us to:

> Give unto the LORD the glory due unto his name; worship the LORD in the beauty of holiness. (Psalms 29:2)

He did not mean that one must be in a beautiful church structure to worship, for he often worshiped on the hillsides and in caves. Neither did he mean that our worship is acceptable only when it comes from high emotional experiences, for David worshiped when he was in the midst of despair. He did feel, however, that worship must flow out of a life that has received a measure of God's holiness.

This Prodigal Son was showing a total lack of holiness. Praise, rejoicing, and worship returned to his life when he chose to abandon this depraved life-style and return to his father. He had a total change in position, and this generated a completely different set of responses. He could worship again because he was back home with his father. So can we if we will return to the Father's house and presence.

I'm Worshiping Again because I'm Restored

It is obvious that a change in position is necessary to return to worship after we have departed from the Father's house, but it should be equally apparent that we also need a change in our condition. The Prodigal Son moved from the foreign pigpen to his father's farm, but his condition was deplorable. He was physically emaciated, his clothes were tattered and his self-esteem was at an all-time low. Before expecting any responses that could be interpreted as praise or worship, the father clothed his son, restored his position in the family with the family ring and fed him at the banquet. Father knew that until the condition of his son was changed, there could be no positive response from him.

This is exactly what God does to a returning son or daughter. He cleanses us from the defilement of sin by the washing of the water of the Word. He clothes us with garments of righteousness to replace our tattered raiment. Then He gives us the seal of the Spirit (family ring) to assure us that we have been received back into full family relationship. He also offers us an abundance of spiritual food to overcome our malnutrition.

In speaking of Israel as being a castaway baby, God said that He found him and gave him life. God said through Ezekiel:

> Then washed I thee with water; yea, I throughly washed away thy blood from thee, and I anointed thee with oil. I clothed thee also with broidered work, and shod thee with badgers' skin, and I girded thee about

with fine linen, and I covered thee with silk. I decked
thee also with ornaments, and I put bracelets upon thy
hands, and a chain on thy neck. And I put a jewel on
thy forehead, and earrings in thine ears, and a beautiful
crown upon thine head. Thus wast thou decked with gold
and silver; and thy raiment was of fine linen, and silk,
and broidered work; thou didst eat fine flour, and honey,
and oil: and thou wast exceeding beautiful, and thou
didst prosper into a kingdom. (Ezekiel 16:9-13)

We hardly reach the corner of the family farm before the
Father begins this change in our condition. He, better than
we, knows how important this change is before we can again
become a worshiper. He understands how impossible it is for
us to worship when all attention is focused upon ourselves.
When our self-image is low, it dominates our attention.
Similarly, when our bodies are weak or ill, it is difficult to
release our spirits in true worship. Often God meets our needs
so we can refocus our attention upon Him.

When the son left the farm, he displayed much of his
father's nature, but the more he lived away from him, the
less he behaved like his father. Correspondingly, when
anything separates us from nearness to God, we lose much
of His nature, for none of that nature is inherent to us — we
receive it from Him. The longer we are away from Him, the
less we think like Him, act like Him or love like He loves.

This impedes our worship seriously, for true worship is
love responding to love. Worship has its origin in God. As
we become aware of His love for us, we receive and respond
by offering some of that love back to God. This allows God
to be worshiped with His own, pure, eternal love. It is
worship at its highest level.

After a season of separation from God, we even lack
self-love, so how can we worship God? He mercifully
receives us back with open arms. The hug and kiss reassure
us of His love, and before long, we respond to Him with hugs

and kisses. We are loving God with His love. We are worshiping again as the Lord promised through the prophet Isaiah:

> The ransomed of the LORD shall return, and come to Zion with songs and everlasting joy upon their heads: they shall obtain joy and gladness, and sorrow and sighing shall flee away. (Isaiah 35:10)

When God's people make the effort for a change in position, God assures them of a change in condition. It seems to be a case of: "I will, if you will." God does not come to the pigsty, but when we come to the farm, He removes every trace of the pigs from our lives.

As we emulate the Prodigal Son in the long walk from the foreign country back to the farm, we, too, formulate our speeches of repentance, but we quickly learn that our heavenly Father accepts the act of returning as repentance. He is not interested in all the details we are prepared to give Him. He is too busy changing our condition to make us comfortable back in the family.

Whether we have gone but a short distance or a long way from God's presence, we consistently need to do a 180-degree turn and come back to the Father. The Psalmist assures us that the first step in worship is to deliberately come into God's presence. He wrote:

> Enter into his gates with thanksgiving, and into his courts with praise: be thankful unto him, and bless his name. (Psalms 100:4)

This change in position will assure us a change in condition that will enable us to worship anew. We can be comfortably assured that, "He restoreth my soul" (Psalms 23:3). Our prayer should be, "Father, it's me, wanting to worship again. Restore me to my old relationship with You."

I'm Worshiping Again because I'm with Father

There is nothing to equal being in the presence of a loved one. Phone calls are good, letters are appreciated, but nothing equals the joy of being with them. My grandchildren tell me that my just being with them makes their Christmas "the best ever." I feel similarly when I can be home with my wife.

How often we Christians try to stir up emotions of love with which to worship God when all we really need to do is come back to His presence and stay awhile. One of David's songs said:

> Thou wilt shew me the path of life: in thy presence
> is fulness of joy; at thy right hand there are pleasures
> for evermore. (Psalms 16:11)

While the Prodigal Son was glad to get back to the farm and appreciated the change in his condition, the true joy was not geographic or physical. It was relational. He was with his father again.

Similarly, as wonderful as our removal from sin is, and as exciting as our change in condition has become, the true joy that incites us to worship is just being in the presence of the Father. As the sons of Korah sang:

> For a day in thy courts is better than a thousand. I
> had rather be a doorkeeper in the house of my God, than
> to dwell in the tents of wickedness. (Psalms 84:10)

One day in God's presence is superior to a thousand away from Him. As the Prodigal Son determined, it is better to be a servant in God's household than anything this world can offer us. God's presence is our ultimate joy.

Throughout the Bible, whenever a person has had a revelation of the presence of God, the immediate response

175

was worship. This was true even when the person was a heathen king. There is something about God's presence that overflows into our lives and gives us a worship experience. We overflow with His love, spill over with His goodness and find ourselves inundated with His mercy. It would take far more effort not to worship God than to worship Him.

The Prodigal Son, broken, bankrupt and bewildered, found refreshing, renewing and rejoicing in the presence of his father. Nothing else mattered to him. So it is with us and God. He renews our strength, He supplies our needs, and He becomes the source of our everlasting joys. Just a season of communion with Him restores the urge and the ability to worship Him. All the cares of life and the ambitions of our souls are laid aside when we are in the comfort of His divine presence, and all we want to talk about is Him. In speaking of Judah in her better days, God boasted:

> They seek me daily, and delight to know my ways, as a nation that did righteousness, and forsook not the ordinance of their God: they ask of me the ordinances of justice; they take delight in approaching to God. (Isaiah 58:2)

May God say this of us in these days of materialistic selfishness. How He longs to have us delight in approaching His presence in obedient righteousness. Those who do so will find the satisfaction and pleasure they didn't find in the far off country. We will find something new in our inner attitudes, and we will begin to enjoy a transformation in our lives, for Paul wrote:

> But we all, with open face beholding as in a glass the glory of the Lord, are changed into the same image from glory to glory, even as by the Spirit of the Lord. (2 Corinthians 3:18)

Paul expounds the principle that while beholding God's person, we are changed into God's likeness. Time spent in the presence of Father God not only renews our worship responses, but it changes our nature to be a little more like His. The more we behold Him, the more we will become like Him. Like the Prodigal Son, we not only return to the farm, but we return to the Father's nature simply by being consistently in His presence.

I'm Worshiping Again because I'm with Father's Servants

The Prodigal Son returned home and asked to be made like one of the father's hired servants. He probably had sweat, toil and labor in the fields in mind. Instead, he discovered that his father not only instructed the servants to prepare a banquet, but said to those servants:

> Bring hither the fatted calf, and kill it; and let us eat, and be merry: For this my son was dead, and is alive again; he was lost, and is found. And they began to be merry. (Luke 15:23-24)

The *us* and *they* must refer to the servants, for the elder brother never joined in the merriment. It was the father, servants, and the younger brother who were having such a marvelous time of rejoicing.

Being a servant of God is not all work. Even God's workers enjoy seasons of worship that bring them to high levels of merrymaking. The angels in heaven are charged with heavy responsibility, yet we read of them rejoicing over conversions. In the Book of the Revelation, we see them worshiping God with songs, praises and high ceremony.

The son asked to be made like one of the father's servants, and was quickly led to a place of rejoicing and merrymaking. Father God does similarly with us. When we surrender our lives to Him and for His service, we tend to expect solemnity and austerity. Instead, we find ourselves joining the other servants in joyous celebration of God. The Bible calls this worship. What religion passes off for worship is often more like a funeral.

This son could easily have staged a one-man celebration, for his joy of being received by his father nearly overwhelmed him. Still, it didn't seem decorous. He had come to express repentance, but when he got caught up in the celebration of the servants, his inner joy was released without restraints.

Worshiping with fellow servants has a way of releasing us to higher levels of joyful worship. Another's song can override our sorrow. A word of praise spoken in our hearing can replace a thought of criticism. Rejoicing in God quickly dispels the feeling of regret in ourselves. The fellowship we enjoy in worship exaltedly enhances the experience. A congregation singing praise unto God can never be equaled by a soloist. Many voices raised in prayer is far more moving than a single prayer to which all say the "Amen!" Correspondingly, when many people join together to worship God, there is community of feeling, continuity of action, and escalation of intensity. Corporate worship will always give higher expression of worship than individual worship. We inspire one another in corporate worship and we complete one another. Corporate worship does not call for uniformity of action. No, it makes possible a great variety of expressions while maintaining a unity of purpose and a consciousness of God's presence.

Perhaps the Prodigal Son was learning what we need to learn. Serving involves worship, and worship involves serving. Just as "all work and no play makes Jack a dull boy," so all service and no worship makes a dull Christian. However, *all* song and dance will make a Christian very unbalanced in his or her walk with God.

If creation worships God by consistently functioning in the realm and way God created for it to function — that is, a rosebush worships by producing roses — then we worship best by functioning harmoniously with the pattern God has set for our lives. There is worship in work. There is worship in child raising. There is worship in giving and worship in living.

All worship does not occur in church. Perhaps what happens in church is merely a celebration of worship. The true worship is to be seen in the everyday life of the believer. As Jesus put it:

> If ye love me, keep my commandments. . . . If ye keep my commandments, ye shall abide in my love; even as I have kept my Father's commandments, and abide in his love. (John 14:15; 15:10)

We need to bow in prayer to say, "Lord, it's me again. Teach me to worship You with my life as well as with my lips."

179